THE ROMAN ART OF WAR
UNDER THE REPUBLIC

The Roman Art of War
Under the Republic

MARTIN CLASSICAL LECTURES

VOLUME VIII

BY

F. E. ADCOCK

BARNES & NOBLE INC.

NEW YORK

1960

Originally published by the Harvard University Press : 1940

Photographically reprinted by permission, with minor alterations
for W. Heffer & Sons Ltd : 1960

PRINTED BY LOWE AND BRYDONE (PRINTERS) LTD. LONDON, N.W.10

THE MARTIN CLASSICAL LECTURES

Volume VIII

The Martin Foundation, on which these lectures
are delivered, was established by his many friends
in honor of Charles Beebe Martin, for forty-five
years a teacher of classical literature and
classical art in Oberlin College

PREFACE

THESE lectures, delivered in May 1939, were written before conditions in Europe brought near the danger of war, and I have not altered them in order to be wise after the event or to dissemble any sentiments which I then shared with many others. The present troubles make even more precious the recollection of my stay at Oberlin, a pleasure added to the honour of giving the Martin Lectures. To friends made there I tender my thanks, and also to friends who read all or part of what appears in these pages, in particular to Mr. Charlesworth, Professor Last and Mr. Syme. I trust I have profited by their criticisms and suggestions. Professor Lord has added to other kindnesses by reading for me the proofs of the Index.

F. E. A.

DECEMBER 1939

B

CONTENTS

I
THE MEN

THE topic I have chosen for the lectures which I have the highly prized honour of giving on the Martin Foundation is the Roman art of war under the Republic. I hope you will regard me as not so stupid or so misled or so dull of heart as to wish to be a panegyrist of war. There have been times when honest men have regarded war as the lesser of two evils and times, especially when the world had less means of using wisdom, when there seemed no place for reason. And there have been times, which are not yet past, when it seemed self-evident that if one must engage in war it is better to win than to lose, and in antiquity it was often beyond the power of statesmanship to evade that issue. With a higher ethic, a higher standard of reason, Roman history would have had less to record of wars. But to understand the past, which is one instrument for moulding the present, we cannot fail to take account of what did affect its history. The art of war was, in fact, an integral part of Roman statecraft, and hateful as were some results of that statecraft, it has left an imperishable mark upon the world. The historian may condemn, condone, admire: it is essential that he should understand. The Romans did not in general admire war; still less did they romanticize it: but they understood it, and without appreciating the way they did so, we cannot understand them.

Much admirable learning has been expended on the topography of ancient campaigns and battles, even more on what may be called the antiquities of Roman warfare, on details of organization and equipment. With neither of these fields of study am I immediately concerned, though I am, of course, indebted to the results that have been gained in them. It is my business rather to discuss the way in which the Romans used the means to their hand in the circumstances of their time, and to attempt a judgment upon them as soldiers or sailors and as directors of military power. My purpose is interpretation, and as interpretation must be, in part, subjective, so it must be, in part, hazardous. All I can do is to give you the picture that has formed itself in my mind, without asking you to accept it when your own judgment does not find it acceptable.

The Roman art of war depended, first, on the quality and quantity of soldiers and sailors that were available, and, second, on the physical setting of their employment, whether on land or sea, and I shall first treat of these topics. Then, as foreign policy and strategy in the larger sense are linked together, I shall try to estimate that side of Roman statecraft, leaving to my last lecture what most people find most interesting, that is, generalship, the higher leading and handling of forces in the field. I have limited myself to the history of the Roman Republic down to the battle of Actium, which may be taken as starting, for this purpose, the Roman Empire. Augustus remade the Roman military machine, set it to work in what was mainly a new geographical setting, and gave a new purpose to Roman statecraft. All these factors affected, if they did not wholly change, the character of Roman generalship. The limitation of time, therefore, though it is imposed by the practical need of finding a manageable topic, is not purely arbitrary or illusory. Even a new deal distributes the same cards, but let us be content to examine how Rome played the hand that Fate had dealt to the Republic.

The genius of the Greeks — I do not now speak of the Macedonians — was, in general, civilian. Apart from mercenaries, very few Greeks were nothing but soldiers, brilliant as were their occasional achievements in the field. Where, as in Sparta, war was a first preoccupation, you had an army which for two centuries outmatched the other Greeks. When Greeks did give their minds to war they were as inventive as in all other things that engaged their intellectual interest, subtle, versatile, alert. On the whole the Greeks made more innovations in tactics and technique than the Romans. But they were not so effective in the long run. Battles are sometimes won by generals; wars are nearly always won by sergeants and privates, and when Rome might be short of brilliant generals she could produce centurions and privates of a peculiar virtue for war. Also she made war in a way which gave scope to her especial advantages. A Roman was half a soldier from the start, and he could endure a discipline which soon produced the other half.[1] To him war was not romantic nor an intellectual adventure: it was a job of work, to which he brought a steady, stubborn, adaptable, schooled application. Roman warfare did not advance with the seven-leagued boots of genius; it marched on, sometimes stumbling, sometimes slipping, but in general it arrived. It was guided not so much by applied intelligence as by applied instinct, but it was not stupid. However, the first thing to consider is what kind of soldiers the Romans were, both by native quality and by training, and I shall now endeavour to examine that topic.

When the Roman Republic enters the light of history its army consists of legions of infantry levied from the citizens according to their ability to equip themselves, and a body of cavalry supplied by the best people which was tactically as much mounted infantry as cavalry in the strict sense. This army was led in the field by one or both of the two consuls of the year unless the stress of some emergency caused the appointment of a Dictator, who had as his lieutenant a Master of the Horse. Military service was a privilege as well as a duty, and the great mass of the army consisted of landowners and independent peasants. The organisation was gradually improved, and those young enough to bear easily the exertions of active operations were separated off from those who could not fairly be expected to do more than defend the City itself. What is called the Struggle of the Orders meant for warlike purposes the gearing-together of all the free elements of the State to meet its needs. Military command ceased to be the monopoly of patricians, and military obligation and political privilege moved together on to a wider basis. Occasional political controversies, rare military mutinies, the clashes of dimly seen economic interests or the immediate sense of economic oppression, the clinging to privilege, all, somewhat distorted by the reflection back of later crises, should not deceive us. Limiting all ambitions, conciliating all sense of grievance, superseding all legalism, the Roman maxim slowly but surely prevailed — *salus populi suprema lex.*

Of the earliest wars of the Republic, fought mainly side by side with Rome's Latin kinsmen, little can be said. We may fairly assume that the Roman foot-soldiers fought in the phalanx, the solid line of spearsmen, a formation probably learnt from the Etruscans.[2] They were mainly concerned to defend the plains near at hand, to repulse or pursue their Etruscan or mountain neighbours. It is possible that the Romans were rather more methodical, rather more farsighted, than others in their warfare. They met the need for occasional longer campaigning by introducing pay for the troops during active service, but the legions remained, as far as we can tell, a citizen militia not so very different from the troops of their neighbours. Then, early in the fourth century, came the great disaster of the Allia, when the Gauls swept away the Roman levies and went near to breaking the Roman State. When the

storm had passed, the Republic set itself to rebuild
and increase its military strength and, after two
generations of experiment, formed the army which
was to win the mastery of Central Italy. By the
time that mastery was achieved, Rome had learnt
what Gallic and Italian enemies could teach her, and
we can at last form some picture of the Roman army
and of the character of the Roman soldiers which
can be deduced from that picture.

At this point I must take up a question which has
been a matter of much controversy.[3] I do so because of the light it throws on the character of the
Roman soldier of the time. How did the Romans
during the middle Republic actually fight in battle,
once the legions had been subdivided, as they were
by now, into maniples or units of about 120 men?
On this we are reduced to the interpretation of pas-
sages in Polybius and a chapter in Livy which has
darkened counsel.[4] The battle pieces of that admirable man of letters do not reveal just what we
want to know. What I believe to have happened is
this. A battle was begun by light armed skirmishers,
the *velites*, whose main task was to cover the advance
of the heavy armed infantry which formed the main
strength. The heavy armed infantry was arranged in
three lines, the first line probably six men deep, the
third three men deep. The first line was called the
hastati, despite the fact that they had ceased to be
armed with the *hasta*, the thrusting spear; the second
line was called the *principes*, despite the fact that

they had ceased to be the first line, which is what *principes* should indicate; the third line was called the *triarii*. The first two lines were armed with a sword and one or two *pila*, the *pilum* being a rather heavy throwing spear with a range of something under 30 yards. The *triarii* were armed with a sword, but with the thrusting spear, not the *pilum*. So far all is agreed ground. At this point doubt begins. It is generally agreed that the maniples of each line were arranged on the parade ground in a chess-board pattern, so that between each maniple there was an interval as wide as a maniple and so that the second-line maniples covered the intervals in the first line, and the third-line maniples covered the intervals in the second. The troops were trained to advance in this way, and then the maniples of the first line were taught to retire and those of the second line to advance, so that the intervals in the first line were filled up. The whole two lines were then taught to retire and to break in such a way as to pass through the intervals between the maniples of the third line, the *triarii*, who advanced slowly with their thrusting spears levelled. When the *hastati* and *principes* had passed through the intervals, the maniples of the *triarii* extended outwards and presented to the enemy a continuous row of spears. So much for the parade ground. The question is what happened in an actual battle.

If we assume that this exercise was practically applied in battle, then I think we must suppose that the maniples maintained their intervals, though of course not necessarily with exact spacing, and the Romans first engaged parts only of the enemy's line. I am assuming that the enemy were drawn up in a continuous line as was the regular practice in other armies. If the enemy were Gauls, whose attack was a rush, then the enemy would filter into the intervals but be held up by the covering maniples of the second line. If the enemy were a phalanx, which depended on a continuous alignment, the parts of the enemy that faced an interval could not advance into it without dislocating their line and exposing the spearmen, who could only fight straight forward as it were, to the activities of the Roman swordsmen. The whole effect so far was defensively elastic. The attack of the Romans began with a short charge of the *hastati* of the front line prepared by one or two volleys of *pila* with the object of shaking the enemy at the critical moment. It is the method advocated by Stonewall Jackson in these words: 'My idea is that the best mode of fighting is to reserve your fire till the enemy get — or you get them — to close quarters. Then deliver one deadly deliberate fire and charge.'

Then followed the fighting with the sword, while the rear ranks of the first line supplied relief to men who fell or tired (for sword-fighting on foot is hard work), and then when the second line came into play they would make possible a second drive forward. If numbers or fighting power saved the enemy from defeat, and if their pressure became too great, the

Romans retired slowly, wearing down the élan and vigour of the opposing front ranks. By this procedure the first two lines, now united into one, came to a point not too far in front of the third line, the *triarii*, who had meanwhile rested and watched the battle. Then at a signal from the trumpets of the legion, perhaps reinforced by the horns of the maniples, the *hastati* and *principes* quickly retired through the intervals of the *triarii*. Possibly the front rank of the *hastati* and *principes* sacrificed themselves to hold up the enemy attack while the rest of their comrades carried out their orderly retreat. For a short interval of time would be needed to enable the *triarii* maniples to extend their ranks laterally after the escape of the *hastati* and *principes* so as to form a continuous line. The enemy, whose leading men were tired with fighting, were now faced by fresh troops who held their ground if they could, knowing that they were the last hope of victory. The *triarii* were the representatives of the older kind of fighting, that of the phalanx, and the Romans thus brought in an old world of fighting to redress the balance of the new. The line of the *triarii* was only three deep and spaced out at sword-fighting distances, so that their steadiness was all-essential, though we may suppose that the *hastati* and *principes* supplied some physical as well as moral support from the rear.

This tactical recipe could not, of course, command certain victory any more than any other, but it did secure the maximum use of the fighting power and expertness of the Roman legionary; in the event of victory, it preserved from loss the *triarii* who were the older soldiers, the fathers of families, whose death would be a greater social if not military loss, and in the event of defeat it gave the surviving *hastati* and *principes* a good chance of escape. In return it demanded the exhibition of peculiarly Roman and Italian qualities, steadiness, self-confidence, strict obedience to command. It had to be practised by the Italian allies as well as the Romans, and demanded like qualities in them. Apart from defeats inflicted by a general of genius like Hannibal, Roman reverses were usually due either to the fact that in a sudden encounter battle the recipe could not be truly applied or to the failure of ill-trained troops to carry through this scheme in the face of a vigorous attack. Reverses from both causes were not rare. Until the last century of the Republic the Romans were comparatively ineffective in scouting and might be caught on a terrain that rendered their deployment difficult so that they were not able to dictate the course of the engagement. Also at times when armies had to be improvised or when armies had bad generals, discipline and training might fall short of the needs of these tactics. But what concerns me here is to point out how these tactics are adapted to the Roman and Italian character which made them soldiers of a stamp unmatched before Alexander, except among the Spartans.

Now if a battle was lost, provided it was a set

battle and not an encounter or surprise battle, the
Romans had a fortified camp into which to retire,
and this brings me to consider the Roman camp in
relation to the character of the Roman soldier.

The habit of a Roman army of not merely encamp-
ing but of fortifying a camp every day, a habit to
which no other ancient army was addicted, needs
some defence however much we take it for granted.
If it mattered how soon a Roman army reached its
objective, clearly it would reach it later if this habit
meant, as it did, that the army marched from a very
early breakfast till about mid-day and spent the whole
afternoon constructing a camp and the whole eve-
ning recovering from its exertions. In order to mitigate
the sense of irrationality that this process might suggest, I will just observe that Roman warfare before it
reached its culmination at the end of the Republic
was unhurried if unresting. Further, the Greek
practice of finding a halting place where nature provided security was apt to waste time also. Further
again, the excavations of Professor Schulten in Spain
have shown that the Romans did not make their
camps schematic in defiance of the terrain.[5] But
what matters most for my purpose is that the camps
were so devised as to maintain at their full value the
Roman virtues of regularity and order. There is
something more than that. There is one sentence
common to the Field Regulations of England, France,
Germany and Russia, and it is that the worst billet
is better than the best bivouac, and it has been ob-

c

served that in the Franco-German War both sides took risks to get their troops into billets.[6] The point is that a sense of comfort and security when not fighting is most important for the *morale* of troops. The advantage of the bivouac, its one advantage, is that the troops are kept concentrated. The Roman camp combined the advantages of billet and bivouac. The troops remained organized and ready for movement; at the same time, as Polybius points out,[7] the wide spaces left free between the walls of the camp and the hutments or tents kept the men out of range of enemy missiles. The battle tactics I have described demanded that each Roman unit should be kept highly self-conscious and at the same time in combination with the other units. This feeling the order of a Roman camp kept awake and aware. Its routine may have dulled initiative, but it gave a sense of security which must have saved the nerves of the soldiers, and also it kept them constantly within the range of discipline.

The leisure hours that followed the completion of the camp were devoted to what the Romans called *corpora curare*, a not uncharacteristic description of the way to spend spare time.[8] But what the Romans aimed at was comfort not only of body but of mind. It is not easy to reconstruct the normal psychological make-up of the ordinary Roman or Italian of the Republic. Some degree of excitability there must have been in a race that was not ashamed of its emotions. Even among the aristocracy there was not the tradition of impassivity — 'that repose which stamps the caste of Vere de Vere.' But in military matters the Romans plainly set great store on a steadiness and coolness of temper which might lack élan but which was needed if Roman battle tactics were to be a success. Those tactics, as we have seen, envisaged retreat as well as attack. The Roman soldier was kept free from nervous strain as long as possible, and the fortified camp was an excellent means to this end. On the other hand, the camp might become a danger if it lured troops to retreat, and it was a shrewd calculation that interposed the third line of old steady troops armed with pikes between the more actively manoeuvring forces and their own camp.

To pursue further the habit of mind inculcated in the Roman soldier, the existence of the camp and the tradition of defending it meant that a Roman army did not over-readily accept defeat. In a battle fought between Greek armies in the classical period, the troops, wound up as it were by the preliminary exhortations of their generals, fought as hard as they could in one continuous effort until one side began to give ground. When this moment was reached (what a Greek poet called 'the turn of battle'[9]), the weaker army broke and set out for home as quickly as possible. A Roman army did not so much run away to fight another day as retire to fight again that day if it came to that. If we may trust the results of battles as described by the Roman annalists for the period of the middle and later Republic, it was seldom that a Roman reverse meant complete disaster.

But what I am concerned with here is what may be called the psychological stiffening of the Roman troops. When the Romans suffered defeats the fault was readily looked for in the discipline of the soldiers, and the ablest Roman generals were reluctant to try to reverse the verdict of fortune until the old confidence derived from strict discipline was fully restored. What is further to be observed is this. Many armies have been successful by mixing together in the same units men of varying degrees of experience and aptitude for fighting. In time of war first-line troops are filled out with reservists at one end and by drafts of recruits at the other, and the attempt is made to fuse together the military qualities of each type. So far as we can reconstruct the practice of the Roman Republic, efforts were made, in the Roman part of the armies at least, to have the main personnel of the legions uniform in age and experience. There seems to have been a great reluctance to weaken the homogeneous fighting value of experienced troops in order to strengthen the fighting value of less well-trained units.[10] What are called 'urban legions' in the history of the third and second centuries B.C. appear to have been formed of recruits who are kept out of the field until they have reached a certain level of homogeneity.[11] Whether a like attempt was made to preserve homogeneity in the contingents of the allies, i.e. the Italians who fought with the legions, we have no means of judging, except that Polybius [12] says that their enrolment was in the Roman method, but as Roman battle tactics implied a certain degree of training in the allies as well as the legions we may assume that the allied contingents were treated in something of the same way.[13] On the other hand, at least from the Second Punic War onwards, there were men who made soldiering their profession and supplied the centurions who were the backbone of the legions.[14]

This brings me to another topic, the social character of the Roman armies. It has been observed how the English armies of the eighteenth century consisted of professional troops commanded by gentlemen.[15] The privates, the corporals and the sergeants came from one class of society, the officers, from the youngest ensigns upwards, from another. The smallest unit in the English army that could act in any way independently was commanded by a young gentleman, and the man who had entered the army as a private and had distinguished himself in twenty campaigns remained this young gentleman's subordinate. This arrangement in fact worked very well, and in an army which was very conscious of class distinctions, an army which dearly loved a lord, it produced a pretty solid *esprit de corps*. In the Roman army the aristocratic officer class was small. The gentry supplied the legion commanders and in each legion there were a number of *tribuni militum* who also were of the gentry. A *tribunus militum* might be set to command some detached group, but when the legion fought as a whole, as it practically always did, the leadership of its several tactical units was vested, not in aristocratic officers, but in experienced soldiers of the social class of the private. Young Roman gentlemen as a rule passed their apprenticeship in the cavalry, not in the legions, and they received no military command whatever till they had reached a comparatively mature age, and their place was as generals or staff officers but not as commanders of the smaller tactical units. Thus what mattered most in the Roman conduct of a battle, its tactical performance, was left in the hands of men of the social class of the ordinary legionaries, who lived with their men, who had to maintain themselves in part by the rigorous Roman discipline but equally by their professional competence and bravery and endurance in the field. The Roman legionary did not carry a marshal's baton in his knapsack, but something more encouraging of effort, the centurion's stick,[16] which marked his authority if need be on the backs of those who came to serve under him. It is to be remembered that down to the last century of the Republic the legions were recruited from peasants who belonged rather to the middle than the lowest class in society, serious folk who took war seriously as they took everything else, and they were offered the chance of a career in which there were many prizes if not large ones, with a limited but realizable ambition to be achieved by competence and courage under the eyes of men of

their own class. Polybius had observed this when he
described the centurions of the middle Republic as
'not so much bold and adventurous as men with a
faculty for command, steady, and rather of a deep-
rooted spirit, not prone prematurely to attack or
start battle, but men who, in the face of superior
numbers or overwhelming pressure, would endure
and die in the defence of their post.' [17] Thus the most
characteristic Roman form of tactical command embodied the virtues sought and usually found in the
Roman soldier. You may remember the maxim of
the Old Buccaneer in George Meredith — 'Steady
shakes them.' On one occasion in the Roman Civil
War 200 veterans save themselves, 220 recruits surrender only to be massacred. 'Here might be seen,'
writes Caesar, 'what security men derive from a resolute spirit.' [18]

But when all is said about the centurions, the Roman armies of the middle Republic remained largely
unprofessional. Legions were raised and disbanded
again after short periods, and the fact that the Roman legionaries were drawn from the independent
peasants meant that most of them were anxious to
return to their farms. The Italian allies, the *socii*,
were probably enlisted from the same class, even if
they were at times kept longer in the field because
they had less influence to back their wish for disband-
ment. Where, as in Spain under the elder Scipio
Africanus, the troops were kept under one general
in one region for several years, it was possible to make

tactical advances, but these seem to have been lost in the second century because these conditions were not repeated. The centurions and soldiers who made arms their livelihood, re-enlisting again and again, supplied a professional element, but it was not until towards the end of the second century that this element became dominant. This brings me to discuss the change that came over the Roman soldiery when the armies became more wholly professional in character.

When Marius towards the close of the second century B.C. enrolled citizens who were not independent peasants, he enrolled soldiers who had no future except with the army, and so from this point the Roman legions became definitely professional. More than that, he appears to have given the legion a kind of personality [19] and from his time onwards the loyalty of the soldier is engaged to his legion, which, with its number, becomes something more definite than it had been. A further loyalty, based on a community of interest, was aroused between the legionary and the general under whom he served. The Roman State undertook no responsibility for the soldier when his service was over, but only did for him what his general could exact, or merely allowed him to receive what his general could confer in the way of bounties when a campaign was over. Thus the soldier looked to his general to keep him serving and then to procure the final payment or grant of land which constituted his pension. [20] I shall have more to say of this under the heading of generalship, as it was an important factor in generalship in the last decades of the Republic.

A further change which affected the character of the soldier was the emergence of the cohort — a body about equivalent to a battalion — as the tactical unit. This had been foreshadowed as early as Scipio Africanus, but it probably did not reach its full development until some time after Marius' reforms.[21] Its effect, when it was fully reached, was to increase the self-reliance and tactical versatility of the legionary. With this went a greater skill in fighting and a greater adaptability to tasks of all kinds, including engineering and even craftsmanship. Thus there gradually came a change which made the Roman soldier more a professional, more closely attached to his general and more immediately dependent in battle on the initiative as well as the steadiness of his centurion. How far this change at first affected the allies, the *socii*, who fought at his side we cannot estimate, but it must have had an effect, and when, as a result of the crisis of the Social War, early in the first century, the distinction between the Italian allies and the citizen legionaries disappeared, the whole Italian *personnel* of the Roman armies became a homogeneous infantry of the line, professional in character and loyal to its professional chiefs rather than to the Roman State. Yet it must not be supposed that it was a mere *soldateska*. It retained its Italian-Roman character, it felt itself superior to mercenaries and auxiliaries, and it kept those qualities of steadiness and discipline under generals whom it trusted. Its centurions, though they might spend the best years of their lives in the field, yet looked forward to becoming men of standing when they retired, though they, like the common soldiers, were ready to return to their profession at the call of their own generals or other generals of reputation. Once fully trained, these troops of the late Republic were perhaps the finest soldiers the world has seen, and after the final schooling in fighting against their fellows in the Civil wars, they passed on to the Empire a military tradition which Augustus knew how to transmute into steady loyalty to the *princeps* and thus to the State.

Thus far I have endeavoured to estimate the peculiar quality of the Roman soldier during the course of the Republic. I must now turn to the matter of quantity and say something about Roman man power.

In the early days of the Republic Rome seems to have been more populous than other Latin States, the Latin States in turn more populous than their Italian neighbours.[22] By shrewd alliances with her neighbours, the Latins and the Hernici, Rome shielded herself to the south and the east, and by her position as the guardian of Latins against the Etruscans ensured the loyal support of her allies in return for making good a limited though vital frontier. So long as the Roman People was united, Rome was strong enough for this task, and with enemies at her doors she was not disposed to shirk it. On the other hand, the need to use the full fighting power of the State, and the manifest advantage to every Roman of seeing that the State was successful in the field, induced, as I have said, Roman patricians to concession and Roman plebeians to loyalty. The danger from the Etruscans waned, but that from the Gauls grew, and the neighbours of Rome, if alarmed by her clear appetite for power, dared not weaken her too far. By shrewd shifts of policy Rome used the Samnites to help control the Latins,[23] and then after equally shrewd concessions, Rome was able to face the Samnites with the Latins and Campanians as her allies.

The contest that ended in Roman predominance in Central Italy was staged as a conflict of the plains against the mountains, and the superior man power of the plains prevailed. Perhaps more by instinct than design, Rome faced each danger to her power with an advantage of numbers on her side. The extension of the Roman franchise kept pace until the middle of the third century with the military needs of Rome. The one thing Rome demanded of her Italian allies was man power. The First Punic War, with its disasters at sea, cost the lives of very large numbers of Italians, but when Rome faced her greatest enemy, Hannibal, she was able to keep an ample margin of strength in the field, and when the Second Punic War ended she was left with abundant reserves of trained men, both Roman and Italian.

The half-century of wars that followed on the north-western borders of Italy and in Spain and across the Adriatic presented new problems of man power for which the Republic did not find a wholly satisfactory solution. Roman statecraft had already contrived to keep in check Philip of Macedon by supporting with Roman troops the forces of other States, and this policy was continued. But it was a cardinal principle of Roman statecraft that Rome herself should match her allies in strength. This principle, which was carried through to the Empire, meant that Roman strength had to grow with Roman dominion. During the second century this principle was endangered by the increasing use of *socii* in the distant wars of the Republic, once the *socii* had less reason to think that their interests and those of Rome were one, and when the discontent of the Italian *socii* came to a head with the Social War, Rome was partly forced to make a wise concession which, by converting Italians into Romans, vastly increased the citizen man power of the State. Thus Rome was able during the forty years that followed the Social War to find armies which extended Roman power as it had never been extended before. Though, largely because of the character of the Roman armies, the constitutional structure of the old Republic was shaken to its fall, the legions made the continuance of Roman power inevitable and by their essentially Western character did much to decide that the centre of gravity of the Empire should remain in the West.

Finally there is the question of the distribution of
Roman fighting power. When I treat of the sea in
my next lecture I shall discuss the extent of Roman
effort on that element. What I want to point out
now is that the Romans regarded infantry of the line
as their peculiar province. They had citizen cavalry
until the end of the second century at least, and
larger contingents of cavalry supplied by the *socii*,
but to them infantry was the queen of the battle-
field. Good cavalry commanders have always been
rare, and cavalry has always been hard to keep efficient. Stirrups were not invented in antiquity, and
without stirrups a cavalryman is rather apt to be like
the White Knight in *Alice through the Looking Glass*,
who always followed up a heavy blow by falling off
his horse. This disability was largely overcome by
other ancient peoples, and some of the great battles
of Greek History were won by cavalry, though not
by cavalry alone. But the temper of the Romans was
in a literal sense pedestrian, and cavalry plays a
small part in the decision of Roman battles. In antiquity cavalry was more used for missile attacks than
for shock tactics, and this effect may not have been
drastic enough for the Romans, and though a few
Roman commanders, especially Labienus (p. 116), did
study the use of cavalry especially in combination
with infantry, it is in general true that horsemen, like
slingers and archers, were largely borrowed from
countries that specialized in them, once Roman political power admitted of it. Thus the essential char-

acteristics of the Roman soldier were preserved, and the legions, especially in their final Republican development, were the staple of the Roman armies.

With Rome the leading military power, and with the legions the predominant arm, the decision of wars rested with them. And this had its ecumenical effect. Had Roman warfare come to depend mainly on cavalry, archers, slingers and javelin-men, the countries which by tradition could supply these troops would have counted more in the ordering of the world. Caesar, the master of legionary warfare, had proved victor over the more varied troops of his opponents, and the fact that the early Empire inherited the military predominance of the legions helped to make the sword of Rome essentially Roman and, with it, Roman imperial power.

II
THE SEA

EVER since Mahan, that distinguished historian who was also a Captain in the United States Navy, wrote his famous treatise *The Influence of Sea Power upon History*, scholars have at times reflected upon the paradox that the Romans, of all peoples the most gifted with an instinct for war, seemingly undervalued so far-reaching a weapon. Not that this generalization is without its exceptions. In his Introduction Mahan singles out the period of the Second Punic War to show how at one period of world history Rome's naval predominance had what seemed to him a decisive influence on the fortunes of that great struggle. But granted its truth, there is much in Mommsen's criticisms of the Romans for failing to realize the advantages of permanent sea power.[1] They were certainly readier to eliminate sea power than to use it: with rare exceptions their strategy only took account of it when its problems were forced upon them. The appreciation of the advantages conferred by sea power so plainly seen in the Greek writers of the fifth century is not reflected in any Roman historian. To the Romans the army, not the navy, was the senior service, as it was, I imagine, to the Spartans. You may remember how in the attack on the Athenians on the beach at Pylos the Spartan Brasidas called on the captains to shiver their timbers on the rocks to get the hoplites into action.[2] That is the authentic voice of the Spartans, who regarded naval fighting as the handmaid of land fighting. So did the Romans. In his life of Antony [3] Plutarch makes a veteran centurion before Actium turn on his general: 'Imperator, why do you think so ill of these wounds of mine and this sword and rest your hopes on wretched logs of wood? Let Egyptians and Phoenicians fight on sea, but give us land, on which it is our way to stand and to die or to vanquish our enemies.'

It has been laid down once and for all by Mr. Justice Stareleigh in Dickens that what the soldier said is not evidence, and what Plutarch makes the soldier say may be romance: but it does reflect the traditional mind of a Roman veteran. When Nero sent detachments from the legions posted in Germany to Alexandria and back, the troops are said to have been so worn down by the sea voyage as to be slow in recovering their vigour of body and warlike spirit.[4] The Roman army, in fact, never got its sea-legs. To the Romans the sea was something incalculable, treacherous. Its calmest moments were a lure and a trap — 'placidi pellacia ponti,' as Lucretius says. It was a sphinx that at times claimed an answer to its riddle, but the Romans preferred evading the sphinx to solving its riddle.

None the less, just as the Spartans went on shipboard if that was the only way, so the Romans took to the sea for the same reason. In 264 a Carthaginian admiral told the Romans that they might only wash

their hands in the sea by his leave.[5] Four years later
the Romans won their first naval battle, and that
over the Carthaginians. It was a Roman general who
coined the dictum that still stands on the doors of
the Haus Seefahrt at Bremen — navigare necesse est,
vivere non est necesse.[6] In the *Bellum Alexandri-
num*[7] the story is told how Caesar's lieutenant Vati-
nius improvised a fleet, manned it with invalid veterans and set out to attack the superior squadrons of
the Pompeian Octavius. 'When he observed,' we
read, 'that he was not a match for the battle in the
size and number of his ships, he decided to trust to
fortune.' Then follows a brisk description how Vati-
nius drove his ship's prow against the enemy flagship
and made it the centre of a conflict which became like
a land battle as the veterans tumbled over on to the
enemy ships and carried them by boarding. It is a
good instance how fortune favours the brave and how
the brave can give fortune a helping hand. Finally
it is not to be forgotten that the last great battle of
the Republic, the battle that decided the issue between Octavian and Antony, was fought at sea off
Actium.

But despite these and other such happenings it remains roughly true that to the Romans the land was
the place to win victories rather than the sea, and it is
also true to say that the Romans sought to conquer
the sea from the land rather than the land from the
sea. In the good old days Englishmen complacently
observed that Britannia needed no bulwarks, no

towers along the steep, and toasted in brandy that had evaded His Majesty's frigates the protective powers of His Majesty's ships of the line. It was not beyond the strength of Rome to guard the coasts of Italy by active squadrons, but, at most times, the Republic preferred to do it by the placing of colonies at strategic points so that an enemy might find himself hampered in movement both along the coast and inland.[8] The sea is *mare dissociabile*, more a barrier and less a road than to the Greeks. As a rule the sea was not the first item in the calculations of Roman statecraft.

When the Roman Republic had a recognizable foreign policy it was concerned with her land frontiers. Down to the end of the fourth century Rome was willing to leave to others effective power by sea and to acquiesce in the limiting of what little sea-going trade Rome enjoyed. Early Rome had hardly any coastline of her own, and when this was harried by the ships of Antium the remedy was not to create a superior fleet, but to force Antium to surrender its ships, whose beaks then adorned the Roman Forum. Livy[9] declares that a number of the Antiate ships were taken into the Roman *navalia*, and it is possible that the statement is true, though years were to pass before Rome set up two officials *duoviri navales* each commanding a small squadron of ten ships. The moral of Antium,[10] as of the prows on the Roman *aes grave*, was not so much that Rome proposed to rule the waves as that the Republic would see to it that no

near neighbour did so, which is a different matter.
When in 311 the *duoviri navales* were appointed, their
purpose seems to have been to assist land operations
by helping communications with Campania. During
the next fifty years little enough is heard of their do-
ings, and it may be conjectured that they were only
appointed when Rome needed a few ships for some
particular purpose.[11] Rome had been content to bind
herself not to send ships into the waters which Tarentum claimed to control, until a duoviral squadron appeared off Tarentum, possibly to assist a *coup d'État*
in the interests of the Republic. If there was such a
project, it failed and the Tarentines made short work
of half the Roman ships. The Roman answer was to
send an army to take order with Tarentum, and
when this led to the intervention of Pyrrhus Rome
made a treaty with Carthage by which it could make
use of Punic sea power rather than create sea power of
its own.

It was not indeed until Sicily, an island yet the
natural extension of the Italian peninsula, forced itself on Roman attention that the Republic faced a
great naval problem. Now with Carthage an enemy
not an ally, control of Sicily was only possible if Rome
could secure access to it by sea for herself and deny
access to an enemy. Furthermore the last word
might have to be spoken before the enemy's capital.
Thus, as Polybius has said,[12] the Romans realized that
victory was only possible if Carthage could be defeated at sea. Willing the end, the Republic willed

the means and rapidly made herself a great naval power. Twenty years of alternating victory and disaster at sea, the latter more often from storms than from the enemy, were a heavy tax on the men and money of Italy. But at last, by a supreme effort, Rome outstayed her opponent, and a final naval victory both isolated the Carthaginians still in Sicily and opened the way for an invasion of Africa which Carthage could not hope to defeat as she had defeated a like venture fifteen years before.

The new Roman navalism was the handmaid of Roman soldiering; and the character of the naval war with its disasters was not such as to turn the Romans into sailors or inspire in them more than a gloomy determination not to be beaten by the sea. The enthusiasm that greeted their earlier victories died away. These Roman successes had been largely won by a device which gave the legionaries a chance of showing their mettle in boarding, and in seamanship the Republic did not set itself to be instructed by its enemies — fas est et ab hoste doceri — and to better the instruction as it so often did in land warfare.

Still less did Rome seek to succeed to the active naval hegemony that had enabled Carthage to make the Western Mediterranean a *mare clausum*. Carthaginian fleets were forbidden to appear in Italian waters, but that was all. Rome did not even impose a limit on the size of the Carthaginian fleet for the future, though we may be confident that any large-scale revival of Carthaginian sea power would have

attracted the hostile attentions of the Republic. A
critical examination of the ancient statistics [13] about
the naval side of the First Punic War has shown that
the normal strength of Carthage at sea was about
130 ships and its maximum strength 200. Rome had
economically outbuilt her enemy as need arose, and
at the end of the war the Roman establishment was
of rather more than 200 ships.

At no time during the Second Punic War did Rome
fail to keep a margin of superiority. Despite occasional enterprises, which must not be underrated, [14]
the Carthaginians could not in that war deny the
Romans the use of the sea or make sure of it for themselves or their allies. In particular, they could not
make up for the naval weakness of Philip V of
Macedon, so that that monarch could be kept in his
place, which was the Balkans. As Mahan points out,
the fact that Rome was strong in the seas between
Spain and Italy made all the difference between
quick and slow reinforcement of Hannibal by his
brother. Carthage could neither support sufficiently
the anti-Roman movement in Sicily nor later be free
from the fear that the Romans might at any time
land a force in Africa itself. At the opening of the war
it was only Hannibal's thrust at Italy which prevented the war beginning and ending before the
gates of Carthage, and when the moment came
for Scipio to cross to Africa it was in easy security.
Yet Roman superiority by sea was not all-pervasive.
Where Carthaginian ships could find a friendly

harbour they might always reach it, if not without risk or in great strength, and the Second Punic War reveals the limitations as well as the range of ancient naval superiority.

The peace that ended the long struggle forbade Carthage to possess more than ten ships of war, and it appears to have become a maxim of Roman state-craft to allow no Mediterranean power to have a formidable fleet which could be used against the Republic. It had been very convenient for Rome that Macedon, largely through lack of funds, had allowed her navy to fall away to nothing, and it has been well observed that one, if only one, factor that made a war-weary Rome act against Macedon at the turn of the century was the news that Philip V was seeking to revive the ancient strength of Macedon at sea.[15] In the Second Macedonian War and that against Antiochus Rome was well served by the fleets of Pergamum and Rhodes, but the Senate was careful not to depend too exclusively upon these allies or to allow their fleets to be too decisive a factor.[16] Twice during the first decades of the second century Rome revived the institution of the *duoviri navales* when small squadrons were needed to keep in check Ligurian and Histrian pirates.[17] But it remains in general true that Rome more and more allowed her own fleets to dwindle, confident that at need she could revive her strength for a major naval war. The converse of this policy is seen in the fact that in the peace treaty of 197 Macedon was limited to six warships and in the peace treaty of 188 Syria was limited to ten warships and these ten were confined to its eastern home waters. Egypt retained a fleet, but a fleet that was only the shadow of her great armaments of the early third century, and Egypt was not likely to cross the path of Rome. It is hardly too much to say that the naval policy of Rome was to avoid the need of having one.

There was no active Roman thalassocracy and no continued effort to police the seas. This duty was largely left to Rhodes, and a malignant Roman policy presently struck at the roots of Rhodian naval power. Before the second century ended the Eastern Mediterranean became infested with pirates, who presented a problem which the Republic sought to avoid solving.[18] Yet the factors for its solution lay to hand, and it is significant what the solution was. It is foreshadowed in an inscription belonging to the very end of the century, in which the Romans enjoin on their maritime clients in the Eastern Mediterranean a policy of denying pirates access to their harbours.[19] It may be that this was one part of some comprehensive operation which was presented by political crises at Rome,[20] but it indicates a line of Roman policy. The seas were to be made safe by the control of the coasts.

This was not a wholly new policy. In the second half of the third century Illyrian pirates had harried Italian trade in the Adriatic. A brisk expedition taught the Illyrians that Rome was impatient of their national industry, and by this and a second campaign ten years later a Roman protectorate was made and maintained on the Illyrian seaboard. More and more maritime colonies guarded the coasts of Italy and were a defence against raiders and also against smugglers.[21] The squadron sent against the Ligurian pirates defeated their ships, but the Roman commanders also sought out on land the steersmen and sailors of the corsairs and put them where they could do no further harm.[22] After the war with Perseus the ships of his Illyrian allies were confiscated,[23] and later a number of expeditions taught the Dalmatians a number of lessons.

But the reluctance of the Senate to add to the provinces of the Republic left to her maritime clients a burden greater than they could bear. The steady weakening of the Hellenistic States made them ill-fitted to endure the occasional demands for ships which Rome made upon them. In the last century of the Republic the forces which these States could supply were relatively small and their mobilization was apparently not easy. When Mithridates challenged the power of Rome his fleets were not as large as might appear from a hasty reading of the ancient authorities.[24] On the other hand it was not without difficulty that ships could be collected to make head against them. Roman provincial governors did little enough to raise squadrons to protect their provinces against piracy, and in the Third Mithridatic War Rome was only spared the necessity of building a new Roman fleet by the dissipation of Mithridates' naval strength after he allied himself with the pirates.[25] There is abundant evidence that small States looked in vain for a *pax Romana* on the seas.

In contrast with this ineffective naval policy may be set the vigorous operations of the Roman general Servilius in the hinterland of Pamphylia and Cilicia, one of the great homes of Aegean piracy.[26] The other great centre was Crete, and here, too, Rome acted, though with less success. At last the danger from the pirates was fully realized. Roman interests which had seen in piracy a branch of the slave trade turned fiercely against a new power that threatened Italy with famine. Lucullus had broken the strength of Mithridates and had done something to build up the naval strength of the client kingdoms. What was needed now was organization and a plan to be carried through by a great concerted effort. Rome roused herself to strike home. An overwhelming group of fleets was gathered together which swept the pirates back to their homes, where Rome completed on land what she had begun at sea. As so often, Rome found the man she needed, this time in Pompey, who, like Agrippa later, understood in a way few Romans did the fruitful interaction of land and sea warfare. He then passed on to consummate the work of Lucullus on land, and his settlement of the East, together with the annexation of Crete and Cyrenaica, completed the other side of Roman policy, the effective control of the Mediterranean coasts.[27] Of naval powers Egypt alone was left, and Egypt and its fleet were Rome's for the taking.

It is not possible to discover what number of Roman ships were built for Pompey's campaign, but when the Civil War broke out the main naval forces in the Mediterranean were those of client states which supported Pompey.[28] Caesar had built some ships to use against Gauls and Britons and was able to have in commission about half as many ships as his enemies once he controlled Italy. As the spread of Alexander's power by land caused the Persian fleet to wither away, so Caesar by his victories on land maimed the sea power of his enemies. This policy was largely forced upon him, but it is significant that the greatest of all Roman generals never tried to control the seas and trusted to chance and daring and the patience of his troops to evade or ward off the dangers inherent in this lack of control. In the campaign that led up to Caesar's victory at Pharsalus Pompey's admiral Bibulus had from 200 to 300 fighting ships and Caesar few, and yet Caesar got seven legions across the Adriatic, and afterwards Antony brought over the rest of the army, though it was only by the luck of a change of wind that he escaped at least severe loss from the galleys of the enemy. None the less, the effect of the Civil Wars of Caesar was to produce once more a head of Roman ships in the west as well as the east of the Mediterranean. On his death Sextus Pompeius, a true son of his father, sought to make himself a power by the naval control of the Western Mediterranean and for a time even threatened to starve Italy. The fleets of the Eastern Mediterranean were predominantly on the side of Brutus and Cassius, and yet Antony and Octavian were able to decide the issue by land at Philippi and to support, in the face of superior naval strength, the largest army which Rome had hitherto concentrated in the field. As the Eastern Roman world passed under the control of Antony he was willing to exchange ships for legions with Octavian, and in the end Sextus Pompeius was worsted by these ships and still more by the new Roman fleet built and organized by Agrippa. When the triumvirs became rivals and enemies, Antony with the financial resources of Egypt built a great fleet to counter the naval strength of Octavian, and the last great battle of the Republic was fought at sea.

Even so, the strategy that led to Actium was more military than naval, and its truest effect was on land. Agrippa's victory over Sextus Pompeius had been attributed to the greater size of his new Roman ships and their effect in a set battle. Antony set himself to match Agrippa's ships in size and numbers and succeeded.[29] With less skilled rowers he could only hope to win at sea by forcing his enemies to stand in his path and fight it out as a kind of land battle. He apparently trusted to his generalship on land to reach a position in which he could fight at advantage on land unless his opponents offered him the kind of battle he might win at sea. Agrippa succeeded in

manoeuvring him into the position in which he had
to fight by sea in order to maintain himself by land,
and with Agrippa dictating the character of the naval
battle Antony was lost. His fleet failed him, and
the campaign on land was thereby decided against
him. The significance of Actium was that it prevented a second Philippi.

With Actium the military predominance of Octavian was assured. The political consequences of
this do not concern us. What matters is that no
power could reach the Mediterranean, which became
for the Empire what it never was for Roman Italy
alone, *mare nostrum*. The Black Sea was still to engage Roman attention, but for the Mediterranean
itself security was assured, even more so than after
Pompey's great sweep, for there are signs of a slight
recrudescence of piracy after that in troubled times.
First three and then two imperial squadrons in the
West, together with a few scattered forces in the Eastern Mediterranean, sufficed to police the seas against
adventurers who could have no safe harbour to
shelter them. With the annexation of Egypt the
last non-Roman fleet disappeared from the Mediterranean world.

After this sketch of Republican naval history we
may retrace our steps and consider the reasons why
Rome with her comparatively negative attitude
towards sea power was so successful in war. First
there are certain factors that apply in general to
ancient naval warfare.[30] Ancient ships of war were

either frail or slow. The Mediterranean does not lend itself to manoeuvre under sail, and such manoeuvre, though precise enough to assist gunfire, is not precise enough for either ramming or boarding. It is significant that the slow-moving great ships of the fleets at Actium were equipped with engines of war, a limited substitute for gunfire.

When ships were frail they had to keep within reach of shelter against storms; when they were slow their range was limited by that very fact. If ships were to be themselves the weapon by the use of the ram, they needed large crews of rowers to acquire the necessary speed and momentum. If ships were to be floating armies they had to carry fighting men whose numbers were greater than their greater size could conveniently accommodate. Thus the complements of ancient ships of war were bound to exceed their capacity for carrying food and water for long. Sailors and marines are patient folks, but to remain at sea for long would leave them over-hungry and over-thirsty. Ancient fleets needed friendly coasts, so that sea power and land power had to go together. When Hannibal held the town of Tarentum the superior Roman fleets could not maintain a blockade of the harbour because the Carthaginian armies could deny them the use of the neighbouring coasts.[31] A close blockade needed *points d'appui* on shore or on some neighbouring island. A long-range blockade was vastly hampered by the difficulty of the fleets keeping station for long at sea. It was never true of ancient warfare that a Grand Army was baulked by 'far distant, storm-beaten ships' on which it never looked. Given a fair start down wind, transports and merchants ships might outrun galleys. They could not be overtaken by the slow and heavy great ships, and if they were overtaken by the frail triremes their solid hulls might bring disaster to their attackers, and a ship manned by few but rowers had hardly the armed men for boarding against a sturdy resistance and certainly not the armed men for prize crews. Naval warfare, in fact, could not earn profits even of hostile crews to be sold as slaves. Difficulties of navigation and signalling tended to keep ancient fleets compact and so limited their range of action. Once darkness had fallen ships of war were blind, and though their prey might blunder into them the chances of capture at night were small. So far as I am aware, once only in ancient history was an army caught at sea in transports and destroyed.[32]

It is perfectly true that in the Aegean world strength at sea was a strong weapon which might guard power as well as trade. In the Western Mediterranean it had given to Carthage some security and much advantage in commerce. In the eyes of those who guided the policy of Rome trade was not always highly important, and I imagine that the weaknesses of ancient sea power as an instrument of war were perceived by men who thought of victory as a goal to be reached by the surefooted march of legions on land. In war sea power works slowly: it is usually partial in its action. Wars have been won on land before the effect of sea power could be felt — witness the Franco-German War, in which the French naval superiority could not affect the issue. 'We English,' wrote Nelson in 1796, 'have to regret that we cannot always decide the fate of the Empire on the sea.' [33] The Romans preferred not to try. We have to bear in mind that though in action fleets of galleys were independent of the wind, they were limited by the fact that the stoutest arms grow weary. As Mahan has said — 'the principles that should direct great naval combinations have been applicable to all ages; and are deducible from history; but the power to carry them out with little regard to weather is a recent gain.' [34]

The point in time at which Rome first took sea power seriously may have affected her naval history. Until the beginning of the third century the standard ship of war had been the trireme, which belongs to the frailer, swifter type of vessel built for manoeuvre and the use of the ram against the side or the oarage of an enemy craft. During the fourth century there had come in the quadrireme, apparently an improved version of the trireme. [35] But the Hellenistic monarchies had by the third century come to trust to larger ships different in type, and the quinquereme had become the standard ship of the line, though fleets continued to contain some of the lighter ships, which were still used in battle. Carthage had followed the Hellenistic monarchies, and when Rome decided to face Carthage on the sea she adopted the quinquereme for her own model. It may be assumed that the Greek coast towns of Italy supplied triremes but the Roman built quinqueremes. These suited the resources of Italy in timber and man power and demanded less skill in the rowers. They also were better fitted than triremes to carry large forces of troops for boarding, and lent themselves to the kind of fighting in which Rome excelled. The device of the *corvus*, a grappling iron to hold an enemy ship during boarding,[36] was the logical consequence of Roman ideas of war at sea.

But the introduction of the quinquereme and still larger ships limited naval tactics, and few States from the third century onwards, except Rhodes, were able to manoeuvre the larger ships with the old subtlety. Thus the development of naval warfare spared Rome the need of acquiring skill to be gained only by long-inherited practice. This fact invited a policy of improvisation and building *ad hoc* and tempted Rome not to develop a continuously high naval tradition. A Roman fleet of quinqueremes could brush aside the resistance of lighter craft, and in battle with its peers the fighting qualities of Roman legionaries were the decisive factor. On the other hand, such a fleet was restricted in range by its comparative slowness, and in Roman strategy the fleets were more employed to break a way for the legions than to gain the command of the sea in a more general way. Such a fleet could cover a slow-moving convoy of transports and supply ships and secure the safe passage of food to Italy when that became a vital interest. In general, Roman naval power was the handmaid of military force or the instrument of hindering the military operations of an enemy. Even so, the Republic was careful to avoid too great dependence on its fleets. Rome preferred marching along roads where this was possible and sought to reach its enemies across a series of stepping stones — from Italy to Sicily, thence to Africa, from Italy to the eastern shores of the Adriatic and thence to Asia Minor. The consummation of Roman naval policy was reached when the Mediterranean could at last be made not so much a sea as a Roman lake.

III

THE LAND

THE Romans came to know warfare by land in a kind of expanding circle. Whatever may have been the activities of warlike kings, the early Republic was concerned with defence rather than attack. The impression conveyed by Livy that the early Republic would have enjoyed unbroken peace had it not been for the ineradicable wickedness of its neighbours is in part due to the practice of the *ius fetiale* which required for a *iustum bellum* a prior attack on Roman life or property. But States find it easy to believe themselves to be on the defensive, and we may conjecture that the responsibility for war was more evenly divided than the Roman tradition would imply. None the less, the Republic was not at first bent on conquering its neighbours. With two of them, the Hernici and the Latin kinsmen of Rome, there was an alliance. North of the Tiber lay the Etruscans, too formidable to be lightly attacked, yet so disunited as not to be a very serious danger. The Sabines were on the whole peaceful; the Aequi and Volscians of the hill country were more dangerous to Rome's allies than to Rome. There was a real military problem to prevent these last from joining hands and cutting Rome off from the Latins, but this was solved in wars in which the triple alliance may have been sorely tried. It is hard to believe that Rome and her associates did not command greater resources of men than these neighbours, and it is significant that no great effort was made to conquer the Volscian hills rather than repel or pursue the Volscians again and again. With the beginning of the fourth century Rome captured Veii and built up a defensive zone north of the Tiber. She was also becoming only too clearly the dominant partner in her alliance which, with the exhaustion of the Aequi and Volscians, was become more an instrument of Roman policy than before. The plain of Latium seemed secure, and the Etruscans were becoming ever weaker. The range of Roman warfare was too short to impose any problem except that of keeping an army in the field for more than a brief summer campaign. This problem had been solved by the introduction of pay where, as was exceptional, long-drawn operations like a siege demanded this kind of effort.

Then came a new and real danger, the attack of the Gauls which nearly destroyed Rome. When the tide of invasion ebbed and Roman power was laboriously restored, there arose the question of the Apennines and their peoples. Whereas it may be conjectured that the more northerly Apennine people were concerned with the Gauls, the more southerly had formed the Samnite confederation, which sought to find homes for a growing population in the lands of their neighbours. Rome postponed the difficult problem of the mountains by allying herself with the Samnites, using them indeed against their old partners the Latins. Then with Campania as an ally of

Rome there began those battles of the mountains against the plains that form the Samnite Wars.[1] The Roman armies, though they had learnt from their defeat by the Gauls, were not yet well fitted to fight in the mountain glens, and it taxed the power of Rome and the Campanians to hold the plains and to block the entrances to them from the Apennines. In this war the Romans, who had already used allies to keep away or canalize, as it were, the dangers that beset them (p. 22), found the advantage of colonies, both Roman and Latin, and showed a strategic appreciation of strong places. They also learnt to profit by the roads that radiated from Rome, not yet the great State-built roads, which began with the Via Appia, but old roads. Along these Roman armies could move more quickly than the hostile forces in the mountains. Gradually after the disaster of the Caudine Forks the initiative passed to Rome, and her armies began to penetrate the Samnite cantons. It is to be observed that they did not seek to seize and garrison Samnite towns but rather to destroy them and devastate the glens: they went a good way towards making a solitude and calling it war. Furthermore, the Romans sought to isolate their enemies by operations and alliances to the north and south of them. The Samnites produced a strategist who strove to break through to Gallic helpers in the north and thence to pass into Etruria.[2] He was matched by Roman generalship, which brought a great army to the point of junction, and the battle of Sentinum decided the fate of Central Italy. The Romans used their victory well and made good the central Apennines as a shield of Rome. Further campaigns solved in drastic way the problem of overpopulation in the southern Apennines, and the Samnites were driven to inactivity which was the equivalent of peace. By the end of the first decade of the third century Rome, enlarged by enfranchisement and strengthened by allies, had made the mountains of Central Italy an asset rather than a liability in its strategy.

This series of operations widened the horizons of Roman strategy and raised the question of the maintenance and supply of armies. Rome was able to use the resources of Campania as well as of Latium, and in the south and east of Samnium the friends of the Republic could provide food for the armies operating in that region. Within the glens of Samnium the Romans no doubt sought to anticipate the maxim of the elder Cato — *bellum se alet*. But even so they must have served a useful apprenticeship in organizing supply by road. River transport in Italy was rarely available, and there is no clear evidence of the use of the sea in this period for the transference of supplies, and even if there was, the real fighting was usually a fair distance inland. The character of the warfare suited the use of comparatively small armies and the normal strength of an independent Roman army became standardized at two legions, a force solid enough to act alone and withstand attack yet not too large to feed and to handle without great difficulty. Compared with the high massifs of Central Italy the south provided few geographical problems. Rome was regarded as the protector of settled life against Gauls and Sabellians and could thus count on the support of some of the Greek towns of the south. The war with Tarentum and Pyrrhus was more a matter of tactics than of strategical geography, though the Roman and Latin colonies did hinder the King's exploitation of his earlier victories. But Sicily in the First Punic War taxed Roman resourcefulness by land as well as by sea. The alliance with Syracuse and the taking of Agrigentum put at the Republic's disposal the resources of Greek Sicily, but the obstinate Carthaginian resistance in the west of the island forced the Romans to organize an elaborate system of convoy by land, in which they proved more successful than their forerunner the First Dionysius.[3] The expedition of Regulus to Africa was even harder to support, and half his army was withdrawn during the winter to ease supply. When the war ended in the complete expulsion of the Carthaginians from Sicily, and when it was followed by the seizure of Sardinia and Corsica, the supply of an army in Africa was more manageable. It is indeed possible that in seizing the latter two islands the Romans were partly at least concerned to facilitate a successful invasion of Africa if need arose.

A different problem was presented by the Gauls beyond the Apennines in the years that preceded the Second Punic War. Armies in this area were too distant to be easily supplied from Rome and for a time at least river transport on the Po would not be safe. On the other hand the country grew abundance of corn of which the Roman legionaries preferred to make their rations, and we may suppose that the Romans collected stores of food in advanced bases of supply. At least Hannibal found such supplies very conveniently collected at Clastidium when he invaded North Italy. In the operations that led to the battle of the Trebia it proved possible to feed two consular armies acting together. In that campaign the Roman defence made use of the rivers of North Italy as many generals were to use them in future times. The strategy of Flaminius in the next year is best explained by the hope of crushing Hannibal by the union of two armies as the Gauls had been crushed at Telamon eight years before. While Flaminius followed Hannibal, who had crossed the Apennines out of reach of him and then marched past him, his colleague Servilius, posted at Ariminum, was preparing to bring his army south. It may be that Hannibal by turning east invited this combination to draw Flaminius into a trap. The Roman general followed opportunity too closely at the heels, and the result was the disaster of Trasimene. Thus the defence failed and the Carthaginians were able to pass south. None the less now, and even after the crushing defeat at Cannae, the strength of the Roman position in Central Italy approved itself. With the help of fortresses, either allied or colonies, which Hannibal could not spare men to take and to garrison, Roman armies were able to hold the field without being forced to accept battle. When Capua, the second city in Italy, went over to Hannibal the Romans were gradually able to cover a successful siege and not to yield to 'Hannibal ad portas.' More than that, it was impossible for the Carthaginians to draw help from Cisalpine Gaul for their army in the south, and the brilliant march of Nero to join his colleague before the Metaurus was possible because the Romans firmly held the central Adriatic coast. Without underrating the political strength of the Roman federation, it may be said that the Republic owed much to its previous strategy in Central Italy and its results. The maintenance of armies in Spain, Sicily and Italy, and finally in Africa, was a training in the technique of warfare. Before Syracuse, for instance, may be seen the Roman appreciation of the advantages of military sanitation [4] and the use of the healthier higher ground, which left the allies of the city to suffer the plague which had been so potent against earlier besiegers of the city. In Spain fleets were used to assist the armies' advance along the coast, and in the Balkans the Romans learnt the art of using overseas allies in the field.

The course of the Second Punic War in Italy suggests that Rome had faced and solved in her own way the problems presented by Italy south of the Po and Sicily. But Spain presented a new area of war. What the Romans were concerned with was the

coastal plain of south-east Spain, the region which
the Carthaginians had come to control. In general
the Spaniards of the high plateaux, apart from the
supply of mercenaries, seem to have left the Carthaginians and Romans to fight it out, and the Roman
victory merely transferred to Rome what Carthage
had held. But in the second century Rome earned
the hostility of the Spaniards, and though at times a
combination of a firm hand and fair dealing secured
intervals of peace, an attempt had to be made to
coerce tribes bordering on the two Roman provinces
of Spain. There is some evidence that the Romans
held a few routes with fortified camps,[5] but the high
plateaux though at times penetrated were not mas-
tered. There were defeats due partly to bad recon-
naissance, partly to bad discipline and bad leadership, until the resolute reduction by the younger
Scipio of the Spanish stronghold of Numantia at
last induced a generation of acquiescence. In the
next century a Roman general, Sertorius, set the Roman government hard problems of strategy. There
had to be a further penetration of the highlands from
the east,[6] but the final solution, the methodical mastering of the whole peninsula, was reserved for Augustus.

Rome's connections with Spain were preferably by
land, and in the two decades that followed the Second Punic War it was necessary to deal with the tire-
some tribes of the maritime Alps, and to restore
Roman authority in North Italy south of the Po.
Livy's account of these events, though it gives a fair

amount of accurate detail, does not make clear the
main lines of Roman strategy, but it would seem as
if Rome was content to get a firm grasp of the coast
and of the plains without mastering the mountains.
The main chain of the Alps was left in the hands of
its inhabitants apparently as a protective screen
against more dangerous enemies. Massilia halfway
between Italy and Spain was protected, and in the
last quarter of the second century the province of
Narbonese Gaul was made to cover Massilia and also
a military road to Spain. The remainder of Gaul was
left untouched though Rome presently made friends
with the Aedui, then the most powerful tribe in the
south of non-Roman Gaul.

On the other hand Rome was less active on her
north-eastern borders. Aquileia, founded in 181 B.C.,
held the gate into the eastern valley of the Po, and
strategic roads made possible the rapid concentration of troops in the north from Central Italy. The
coasts were guarded against Histrian pirates, and occasional campaigns in Dalmatia showed the power of
Rome. But no attempt was made to control that
country or by an advance to Siscia to turn the great
barrier of the Dinaric Alps.[7] The Romanization of
northern Italy, itself slow, was not accompanied by
any farsighted military policy for defence should
a powerful enemy threaten from the north-east.
Towards the close of the century Rome had anxious
moments when the Cimbri and Teutoni appeared in
Carinthia. For a moment after a Roman defeat at

Noreia the way to Italy lay open to the invaders, but the cloud of war drifted off westwards. Here in Narbonese Gaul the tale of defeat was repeated, and once more the enemy failed to follow up their victory. Marius was given time to train an army and prepare the defence in the west. When at last the barbarians did advance on Italy they divided their forces. The Teutoni were to force their way through Provence, the Cimbri to descend on Lombardy from the Brenner, the Tigurini, their allies, to strike at Aquileia from the east.

The Romans made good use of the inner lines.[8] Marius was able to win a great victory in the west while his colleague Catulus, more by luck than judgment, avoided disaster in the plain of the Po, and Sulla watched for the attack from the east, which fortunately failed to be effective.[9] Marius was then able to bring his victorious army into North Italy and inflict a decisive defeat on the Cimbri, who had not passed the line of the Po. Cisalpine Gaul was saved to become a great recruiting ground for the Roman armies, and once more Italy was secure. But Roman strategy in Italy was soon to be tested again. After little more than a decade Rome was faced by the great revolt of her Italian allies, whose strength lay in the Apennines. In the northern half of Central Italy Marius conducted a shrewd defensive, moved, it may well be, by a wise desire to prepare for a settlement by compromise. Farther south Rome had to face much the same geographical problems as in the Samnite Wars and dealt with them in much the same way. To the north-east the Romans kept a firm grip on the region that might link up southern with north-western enemies. The siege of Asculum and the victory that covered the siege may be compared with Sentinum in its effects.[10] By victories, however checkered by defeats, and by political concessions, however grudgingly administered, the Republic contrived to weather the storm.

The conflicts of the next ten years in Italy throw little light on this field of war. The defence of Italy against Sulla returning from the East was confused by pro-Sullan movements in the North, so that he was able to march from Brundisium to Campania without striking a blow.[11] Thence fighting and cajoling, part lion and part fox, Sulla reached and entered the gates of Rome. But to be master of the City did not mean being master of Italy. The operations in Etruria, Umbria and Cisalpine Gaul showed that the military centre of gravity in Italy was moving to the north. It is true that in Samnium there remained implacable enemies of the Republic and that the Samnites had a last fling in a march on Rome, but after their defeat Samnium ceased to be of military importance. The destruction of life in Etruria and Umbria in these wars cannot be measured, but it must have been very great. On the other hand, settlements of veterans by Sulla and Pompey throughout the peninsula meant that any mobilization would be widely distributed. Caesar, who early appre-

F

ciated the military importance of Cisalpine Gaul, was able by his bold advance from Ariminum, in the opening days of the Civil War to transfer to his side troops who might otherwise have joined Pompey, and to drive his opponent from Italy.[12] Both generals fully realized that the possession of Rome itself was the prize of victory rather than the condition of it. The operations that followed the death of Caesar were governed by the same geographical and strategical principles. North Italy was the vital region strategically, once the veterans had been set upon the march.

We may now retrace our steps and consider the attitude of the Republic to more distant theatres of war. The destruction of Carthage led to a Roman province in North Africa. The occupation of what is now Tunisia completed the Roman line across the Mediterranean, but the Senate was then anxious to leave to a client kingdom of Numidia the task of shielding the province from nomads. The Romans were reluctant to adapt their military methods to the problem of African warfare and to assume any larger responsibilities, until the domestic activities of the Numidian royal house forced this upon them. But even when the recalcitrant ambition of Jugurtha had compelled Rome to put an end to him, the Senate shrank from completing her hold on North Africa. Rome was slow to annex what is now Tripoli and preferred to keep client Kings in Morocco and part of Algeria.

Next comes the Balkan peninsula. Partly to secure the Adriatic from pirates, partly to secure Italy from Macedon, the Romans formed and maintained a kind of protectorate to the east of the Straits of Otranto.[13] The ports of this protectorate, lying within easy reach of Brundisium, were then used as the ways of entry into the Balkans, so that the Romans became accustomed to operate against Macedonia from the west, despite the difficulties presented by the country to be traversed. These difficulties perplexed more than one Roman commander, and it needed the co-operation of allies in Greece proper to make Roman action against Macedonia effective. On the other hand Rome avoided being too dependent upon her allies, and after Macedon had been finally defeated, the Via Egnatia from Dyrrhachium to Thessalonica supplied a route for armies to the north Aegean. But the elimination of Macedonia as a great power transferred to Rome an obligation, the duty to shield Greek lands from northern barbarians. Macedon had never been strong enough to subdue the country between the Aegean and the Danube, and was always preoccupied elsewhere. Rome had the strength, but was content to leave the governors of Macedonia to win triumphs with smallish armies without ever facing the major problem of defence.[14] Here and there are signs of greater insight: when Mithridates began to make contacts with the tribes of the lower Danube, Marcus Lucullus, brother of the more famous consul, was sent to occupy their attention. But there is no doubt much truth in Cicero's description of Macedonia as a province whose borders extended no farther than the range of Roman weapons.[15] The late Republic at least must have had the geographical knowledge necessary to show that the Danube was the defensive line at which Rome should aim, but preferred to leave the initiative to the barbarians and be content to hear of victories which never made further victories unnecessary.

Beyond the Balkan peninsula lay Asia Minor, which leads on strategically to Syria. Rome got a footing in Asia Minor by the bequest to her of the Kingdom of Pergamum in 133 B.C. Hitherto the Republic had sought to avoid commitments beyond the Dardanelles. For whatever reason, Rome accepted the legacy but sought to limit her commitments. The province called Asia was to be protected by a circle of client-states whose jealousies would keep them loyal to Rome. But when the ambition of Mithridates upset this variation of the balance of power, Rome had to face the military problem of Asia Minor which the Greeks before Alexander, like the present-day Greeks, failed to solve. For a successful invasion of Asia Minor from the west two things were needed, the power of organizing supply and the power of taking towns or fortified positions. These two things Rome understood, and the *Luculli miles* of Horace remembered his achievements against the royal *castella*.[16] After Lucullus, Pompey carried Roman arms into Syria and strengthened the defences of

both Asia Minor and Syria, now annexed, by the crea-
tion of the strategic kingdom of Commagene to hold
the line of the Euphrates and the entry to both
regions. Roughly speaking, the coasts of Nearer
Asia were made Roman territory, though within this
frame client kings, cities or temple states were left to
govern themselves. But admirable as was Pompey's
settlement in the main, he did not clearly define the
limits of Rome's claims or achieve a thoroughly scientific frontier against Parthia; nor did he appreciate
the strategic importance of Armenia.

The last great region to claim the attention of the
Republic was Gaul, a country of geographical variety.
It was no longer barbarous when Caesar entered it,
and it did not present the difficulties presented by
Spain. The country had roads and also the possibil-
ity of river transport.[17] It was large and populous,
and for its conquest there was needed what Caesar
could supply — strategic insight, great mobility and
skill in defeating an enemy in detail.[18] Much of
Caesar's success is written in the first words of his
commentaries — 'Gallia est omnis divisa. The speed
and completeness of the Roman conquest of Gaul de-
serves the admiration it has received. But even here
the Republic's reluctance to face the difficulties of
mountain warfare may be seen: Gaul was, as it were,
conquered from Marseilles rather than from Rome,
and it was not till Augustus that the Little and Great
St. Bernard, the shortest and most convenient routes
from Italy to Central Gaul and the Upper Rhine, were

freely open for armies and traders.[19] While Caesar was conquering in Gaul Crassus had attempted the invasion of Parthia and failed. His failure showed defects in Roman tactics against a well-munitioned missile attack,[20] and it also showed that deserts could themselves be an enemy. On the other hand, the Parthian Empire was ill-organized to follow up its victory and Syria was held. Crassus' defeat proves nothing about the problem of the right strategy of an invasion of Parthia. How Caesar meant to solve this problem ten years later we do not know, though some scholars write as though we did. Nor do we know how far he meant to press a Roman advance. The operations of Antony later do not settle the matter, for his failure was chiefly due to the almost accidental loss of his siege-train, a loss which took from the Romans the advantage they had in their campaigns in Asia Minor.

Great as was the activity, often enforced, of the late Republic, it is instructive to observe how much was left for the early Empire to undertake. Cyrenaica had been annexed with leisurely deliberation in 74 B.C. Caesar made a temporary settlement in North Africa, and after Actium Egypt was added to the *imperium* of the Roman People. Thus the control of the Mediterranean coasts was complete. But it was reserved for Augustus to make Roman power in Spain coterminous with the Peninsula, to master the high Alps and Bavaria and to incorporate Switzerland and the Tyrol. Equally important was the annexation of Pannonia and the winning of the line of communications that led from Aquileia through Emona, Siscia, Sirmium, Singidunum, Naissus and Serdica to Byzantium, the line now followed by the Balkan Orient Express. Thrace was firmly held as a client kingdom, and Roman arms were advanced through Moesia to the Danube.[21] This was the work of the early Principate. Before Actium Octavian had campaigned in Illyria, but rather to add to the security and to win the gratitude of Italy than as a stepping stone to the advance on the middle Danube.[22] It remains true that Republican Rome thought of war by land first in terms of Italy, then in terms of the Mediterranean, and despite the conquest of Gaul left to the future the military problems of continental, as distinct from Mediterranean, Europe.

There remain two matters that fall in this category of land operations. The first may be called obstacles and their removal, the second movement. Italy is a country adapted to obstacles — by which I mean ways of halting or impeding an enemy's movements. In general its river valleys are narrow, or its rivers are not easy to cross. It is thus a country in which fortresses have always played an effective part, and the Romans, in choosing their allies and in choosing sites for their colonies, showed a shrewd appreciation of this fact. The art of fortification seems for a long while to have kept ahead of the art of taking fortresses. To neither art did the Romans make any great contribution so far as can be told. Admirable engineers as they were, they appear to have borrowed freely from the Greek science of fortification when that developed at the turn of the fifth century. There is indeed some evidence that the fourth-century fortifications of Rome itself owed a good deal to Greek builders from Magna Graecia or Sicily.[23] In the Second Punic War it would seem that the cities in Italy were too strong for Hannibal to take without losses which he could not afford. They provided cover for Roman forces when Hannibal was master in the open field wherever he was in person with his army. What was, however, particularly Roman was the skill with which the places to be fortified were chosen especially to deny to an enemy the use of the main routes in Italy.

It looks, however, as if the long security of the second century led to a neglect of fortresses: at least there is evidence for activity in repairing and improving fortifications in Italy in the time of Sulla.[24] Though direct evidence is lacking, it would appear that the Social War in Italy had made some weakness apparent. As in fortification, so in siegecraft, Rome appears to have borrowed from the Greeks, though the legionaries, with their training, may well have surpassed the Greeks in the speed and solidity of their siege-constructions. With the closing decades of the Republic the Romans seem to have reached a high degree of skill in taking cities or smaller strongholds without too great cost in the lives of their very valuable soldiers. This skill was exhibited in particular in Asia Minor, where the country was dotted with castles and small fortified points. So far as we can tell, there was a marked advance in the technique of bridging rivers between the second century and the time of Caesar. The famous bridge over the Rhine was not an isolated achievement. I do not think, on the other hand, that the Romans were skilful in mountain-fighting. This seems at least a fair deduction from their usual strategy of holding the low countries and rather pinching out or blockading any mountainous area than seeking to master the hills by direct attack.

Next, the question of movement. The rather deliberate character of Roman strategy was not due to lack of mobility in Roman armies, apart from the habit of fortifying a camp. In general, and more and more markedly under the later Republic, Roman armies travelled pretty light. From Marius onwards at least the Roman legionaries could carry a good deal with them, and the transport was organized and subdivided so as to be kept handy to the units it served. More than that, it was in the main carried on pack animals able to go wherever a man could pass. The economy of missile weapons in the Roman practice of battle and the Roman skill in making engines of war from local material meant that the armies were not cumbered by what may be called ammunition and artillery. I have already mentioned the Roman provident care about supplies, and it is to be remembered that Romans were abstemious both in food and drink. The relatively small forces of cavalry which they used restricted the need for collecting fodder, or when they did employ fairly large forces of cavalry these were generally of high quality well able to seek their own supplies. On the other hand, the need for fodder did exist, and this helped to limit campaigning to the summer season. One reason in fact for Caesar's bold decision to blockade Pompey at Dyrrhachium was the desire to weaken his cavalry by limiting the area from which it could get fodder for the horses.[25]

The Romans were good marchers. You may remember the famous aphorism of the Marshal de Saxe — 'in the legs lies the whole secret of manoeuvre and battle.' There is one other dictum of a greater master of war — Napoleon — 'The secret of war is to march twelve leagues, fight a battle, and march twelve leagues more in pursuit.' We must discount some ancient statements of the marching powers of Roman armies, but this is true, that the very best Roman troops could live up to Napoleon's maxim — witness Caesar's veteran troops at Gergovia and at Pharsalus — and on the whole the legs of the Romans did not fail them at need. The comparative smallness of Roman armies helped here: it also helped to avoid wastage on the march, which seems to increase in a geometric rather than an arithmetical progression with the size of the forces concerned. Napoleon's first rule was that two men will beat one, and he performed great feats to bring his two men to-

gether at the right moment. Caesar's first rule was
that one good man will beat two inferior ones,[26] and
though he carried this rule further than other Roman
generals, it would seem that the usual Roman practice was to concentrate on quality and avoid the
friction that is produced by the movement of un-
wieldy forces. I have said that the Romans were not
very good at scouting, but they can be credited with
a firm discipline on the march which would avoid
much wastage except in very difficult conditions such
as attended Antony's retreat from Parthia. We cannot find in Roman military history anything to match
the far-ranging movements of Alexander the Great,
which seemed to mock distance and terrain, or the
brilliant timed concentrations of Napoleon, but
within the normal ambits of its needs the Roman art
of war was in the main well served by the mobility
and endurance of its soldiers.

IV

FOREIGN POLICY AND GENERAL STRATEGY

IN THIS lecture I am not concerned with the ultimate motives of Roman foreign policy, how far, for instance, it was due to economic considerations, but with the use of war to further policy. A famous definition of war indeed is that it is only the continuation of State policy by other means. This implies that policy, particularly foreign policy, may gain its ends without war, that it may succeed in preventing war: on the other hand it can prepare the way for war, aiming at reaching a position favourable to a decision by those more violent means. When this happens foreign policy and strategy are apt to interact on each other. To have to fight as few enemies as possible in order to achieve one's object is clearly a strategical advantage: so too is to have as many allies as possible provided that in war they are assets rather than liabilities. It is a part of a shrewd foreign policy and strategy to foresee whether this will be so. One thing which we must therefore consider is how far Rome had this shrewd appreciation of the way in which her foreign policy would work out when subjected to the test of war.

From the beginning of her known history Rome made alliances which were aimed at improving her strategical position, or, to look at it the other way round, at making worse the strategical position of her present or possible enemies. For example, Rome's alliance with her neighbours, the Latins and the Hernici, limited her strategic liabilities. Between Rome and the Latins there was a sense of kinship, but in general the early alliances made by Rome can be explained as assisting her strategical advantage, and this is usually a sufficient explanation of them. There have been alliances which do not rest on any natural affection, nor even on a general coincidence of interests, but on particular strategic considerations. Such was the alliance between Rome and the Samnites in the fourth century[1], and, as such alliances are apt to be, it was short-lived. A community of economic interests may be a link, but in general ancient States had only a small appreciation of economic interests, and foreign policy was apt to be guided by just such considerations as bring it within the scope of this lecture. Policy may then aim at avoiding war, or at postponing war, or at times at preparing for and even hastening war.

For a long while at least under the Early Republic Rome's foreign policy towards Carthage succeeded in avoiding war by admitting special interests which Carthage claimed; her policy towards the Samnites succeeded in postponing war; her policy towards Philip V of Macedon at the turn of the third century was apparently designed to hasten war. Roman foreign policy towards Carthage in the months immediately preceding the Third Punic War aimed at hastening war and preparing for it.

This is perhaps sufficient preamble to show that

foreign policy and strategy may be connected. Policy can also affect strategy if it determines in advance the objectives of a war or the character of a war. A war may be conducted, for instance, with an eye to quite limited results, results which fall short of the overthrow of the enemy. It may aim at a quick and crushing decision or it may be conducted so as to exhaust an enemy's resources or his will to complete victory. Since Clausewitz, a distinction has often been drawn between what may be called the strategy of overthrow and the strategy of wearing down or wearing out, between war conducted à la Napoleon and war conducted à la Frederick the Great.[2] Some who have made this distinction have found the first kind of strategy concerned to bring on battles, the second to evade battles. This is not quite the same distinction. The object of Frederick the Great was to prolong the Seven Years War and wear down the will to conquer of his enemies, but his method was certainly not the avoidance of battle where battle might serve this end. How far can these distinctions, in which strategy and policy may go together, be applied to Roman military history? In the first year of the Civil War between Caesar and Pompey, Caesar took an army to Spain and secured the elimination of Pompey's army in the Peninsula without actually fighting a battle. None the less he was pursuing the strategy of overthrow: he was no less anticipating strategy of the Napoleonic type because his object was attained without an actual clash of arms, just as the elimination of an army at Ulm was no less Napoleonic than the destruction of an army at Austerlitz. Both Caesar in Spain and Napoleon at Ulm really achieved their ends because they reached a position in which they could be sure of winning a battle if it came to that.

But wars do not always go according to plan, and the political purpose of a war may have to be attained by strategy that (for a time at least) appears not to conform to it. Let me illustrate this whole group of ideas by a brief examination of the three great wars which Rome waged with Carthage. The first war was to secure control of Sicily — that is, it was a war with a limited objective. There is no reason to think that Rome at this time envisaged the final destruction of the power of Carthage. Roman strategy aimed at driving the Carthaginians from Sicily, and for nearly ten years Roman armies operated in Sicily and Roman fleets were busy isolating the Carthaginian armies on the island and securing communications with the island. Then an army was landed in Africa. When Carthage offered to negotiate, the Roman general made impossibly harsh demands,[3] but I believe he went in advance of Roman policy because he wished to win a resounding victory by his own efforts. He met with defeat, and this defeat was followed by two naval disasters due to storms. Rome then returned to her former policy, if she had ever left it. After another ten years the idea of invading Africa was renewed, and when the way to Africa had been cleared by the Roman fleet Carthage gave way. Rome secured her object and did not seek to achieve more except to get an indemnity. In fact Carthage was allowed to find in Spain a new province to compensate her for the loss of Sicily and assist her to pay the indemnity. But the Romans became alarmed at the revival of Carthaginian power and may have feared a Carthaginian *revanche*. Whether Hannibal forced war on Rome or whether Rome forced war on Carthage has been much disputed. Myself, I think the greater weight of responsibility rests on Rome.[4] But what matters for our purpose is the object with which Rome entered the Second Punic War. I do not imagine that when the war opened any Roman supposed that the Republic would have to face a Carthaginian army in Italy. It was not from Rome's point of view begun as a war to defend Italy. Nor was it a war simply to deprive Carthage of its new province in Spain while leaving her strong in Africa. The Roman dispositions at the opening of the war suggest that Rome did not aim at annexing the Carthaginian possessions in Africa but did aim at destroying Carthage as a great power. The army sent to Spain was apparently to contain Hannibal, as the soldiers say, while the decisive blow was to be struck in Africa, probably in the next year.[5] This plan was derailed by Hannibal's march into Italy, and a series of Carthaginian victories put Rome tactically on the defensive. When the Roman confederation in Italy did not break up,

Carthage tried to make a coalition of States in Sicily
and the Balkans against Rome with the object of
confining Roman activity to peninsular Italy.[6]
Either the breakdown of the Roman confederation
or the success of the coalition would achieve the real
purpose of Carthage, to reverse the verdict of the
First Punic War and secure the Carthaginian province in Spain. I doubt if even Hannibal ever, or at
least for long, imagined the destruction of Rome as
an Italian power to be possible.

What did Rome do? In Italy she did what she
could to hamper Hannibal, she contrived by a
shrewd use of her armies and fortresses to reduce
Capua, the one Italian city of the first importance
that joined the Carthaginians. In Spain she continued
her offensive defensive. The first object of this campaign was now to prevent the Carthaginian army in
the peninsula from reaching Italy, the second was to
weaken and ultimately to supplant the Carthaginian
power in Spain. After various ups and downs Scipio
Africanus was sent to Spain. He pursued the second
object — that of weakening and destroying the
Carthaginian hold on Spain — with more success
than the first, for Hannibal's brother did contrive to
reach Italy with an army. This army was defeated
by a brilliant manoeuvre which concentrated two
armies against it while Hannibal was left in cold
storage in the south of Italy. But brilliant as it was,
this manoeuvre was a tactical interlude in the major
strategy of the war. In Sicily the Romans restored

their power; in the Balkans, by a shrewd alliance and slight military exertions, they kept King Philip of Macedon at arm's length until he made peace.

After thirteen years of war the Carthaginians had practically lost Spain: their coalition against Rome had broken up, and Scipio proceeded to Africa to deliver the *coup de grace*. With an army trained in new tactics and allied with an African prince, he put Carthage in the position of having either to yield or to try the last chance of war with Hannibal's army brought from Italy. Carthage did in fact try to yield, but Hannibal returned and brought on a decisive battle in which he was defeated. Carthage had to surrender, and the terms of peace reduced her to a third-rate power. So ended the Second Punic War. What I want to point out is that if you take particular areas of this war, as in the Balkans, or particular periods, as that immediately following Hannibal's series of victories in Italy, you might say that Rome was pursuing the wearing-down strategy. But if you take the whole course of the war you must, I think, suppose that Rome never really abandoned her original purpose of destroying Carthaginian power, that, in fact, she was pursuing the strategy of overthrow from start to finish. Even her diplomatic and military activity in the Balkans, though it did not aim at destroying Philip of Macedon, did have an ulterior object of destroying Hannibal and the power of Carthage.

It is possible that at times Rome did come near to

abandoning her designs and that the famous Fabius may have been disposed to be content with a successful defensive. I judge this not from his Fabian tactics so much as from his opposition to the expedition to Africa while Hannibal was still in Italy.[7] The slogan 'peace in Italy before war in Africa' might have tempted to a peace in which Rome left Carthage a great power in return for the withdrawal of Hannibal from Italy. But the initiative of the elder Scipio and his friends kept Roman determination fixed to its original purpose.

Now let us consider the Third Punic War two generations later. The purpose of Rome was now the destruction of Carthage not as a great power but as a city at all. The reasons, all pretty unworthy ones, that induced this decision do not matter for our purpose. For whatever reason, Rome had decided that Carthage must be destroyed — '*Carthago delenda est.*' And now we see Roman diplomacy busy to prepare for the decisive blow. No concession that Carthage could make could save her, and the Roman demands were simply so many advance operations of war. Here in its most drastic form you have diplomacy and foreign policy serving the ends of warlike strategy. By a crime rare in the annals of history Carthage went up in flames, and the younger Scipio, the ultimate agent of this hateful policy, was moved to quote to his friend Polybius a famous couplet of Homer —

'A day shall come when holy Troy shall fall
And Priam, lord of spears, and Priam's folk.'[8]

But the punishment that Rome deserved did not come. The day of retribution that Scipio feared was centuries away. Moral indignation is weakening to historical judgment, though it may properly strengthen and even inspire political actions, so I will not dwell longer on that. What I wish to show is how war can be the end of foreign policy and how diplomacy can be the handmaid of war.

Now let me turn to a general consideration of the character of major Roman strategy and of foreign policy in other fields than against Carthage. The majority of Roman wars cannot readily be divided into wars of wearing down or wars of overthrow, and this is not surprising if the *personnel* and tradition of Roman armies and the Roman attitude towards the problems of sea and land have been rightly interpreted in the preceding lectures. Rome usually took war easily: she did not in general regard it as a violent interruption of her normal life, an interruption that must be ended as soon as possible. This was not because to Rome war was a glorious adventure; it was a necessary evil, but the necessity was to Rome more apparent than the evilness. In the next place, the military virtues of Rome were rather those of tenacity and cool stubbornness than those of swiftly aggressive action. What we have observed in the field of tactics is very often to be observed in the field of strategy. Roman armies were framed to make sure of having the last word, not to try to make the first word decisive, to wait on the mistakes of an

enemy and to wait with the confidence of a well-
tried system and usually a reserve position tactically
in the shape of the camp, a reserve position strategically in a network of fortresses, or the support of
allies. A Roman war often enough is a Roman battle
writ large.

Further, the conditions of Roman command often
meant that the generals at the beginning of a war
were men of mediocre capacity, and the conditions
of Roman armies sometimes, though not so often,
meant that the troops were capable of improvement
and better fitted for tentative than decisive action at
the beginning of a war. Roman generals, once they
took the field, were not hampered by constant interference from the home government. They had not
to resort to the devices of a Marlborough hampered
by Dutch commissioners putting limits on the range
of strategy, even though limits of space were set by
the *provincia* entrusted to a Roman commander.
Many wars have shown the evil results of a civilian
policy imposing either inaction or wrong action upon
soldiers, and some wars have shown the evil results
of soldiers taking too narrowly professional a view
of the needs of major strategy. The Romans had the
advantage that their policy was directed by men with
some military experience and its strategy by men
with some knowledge of foreign policy. In the late
European War soldiers were impatient of statesmen,
statesmen of soldiers; the Roman Senate and the
Roman generals had a tincture both of soldiering and

statesmanship. But the instructed experience of the Senate was ready to be critical of any commander who tried to do too much too quickly, and the sharpest condemnation was reserved for those generals who tried to snatch a victory too hastily from motives of personal desire for distinction. No Roman general would be blamed for achieving too little if his judgment induced him to delay. When at the beginning of the campaign of Cannae the Senate definitely instructed the generals to fight a decisive battle, the Senate took on itself the blame when the result was disaster. It was not just a gesture of magnanimity when the defeated Varro was greeted with praise for not having despaired of the Republic. The phrase meant that he was held justified because he had obeyed orders. But, as a rule, it was the business of a Roman general to do the best he could and to be more concerned to avoid defeat than to achieve victory.

Most of the wars of the Republic in the period for which we have real information were fought not on Roman territory but in hostile or allied territory, and that makes it less disadvantageous to wait one's time. As Jomini has said — 'It is always easy to use Fabian tactics (*faire le Fabius*) when one is in allied territory, when one has no need at all to be anxious about the fate of one's capital or provinces in danger, when indeed one need only take account of what is militarily in place.'[9] Jomini continues: 'To sum up, it seems beyond doubt that one of the greatest talents of a general is to know when to use in turn the defensive offensive and the offensive defensive and, above all, to be able to regain the initiative in the very middle of a defensive conflict.' The Romans had certainly this talent, though it might be brought into play in the change of commanders, or when a general whose instinct was for decisive attack replaced at the right moment a general whose instinct was for defence or tentative measures. We may compare the effect of the appointment of General Grant on the course of the War between the North and the South. For this purpose, during almost all the Republican period, Rome seems to have had an adequate supply of commanders of respectable ability among whom could be found men whose natural gifts suited any kind of strategy. The Senate's authority over the sphere of action assigned to each of the available magistrates may well have enabled it to influence strategy without interference with the judgment of the generals once their sphere of action was allotted.

There is one thing more that inclined the Republic to play a long game, namely, that Rome operated with comparatively small armies. This reduced the degree of pure technique needed in her generals, and it also reduced the effect of any one reverse on the fortunes of a campaign or a war. On the other hand, Rome was in general reluctant or unfitted to produce the concentration of force by which swift, overwhelming and decisive victory is as a rule to be achieved.

Finally, it was a cardinal principle of Rome not to

make peace except after a victory, but the Republic was, on the whole, readily — perhaps too readily — satisfied with a victory that did not destroy her enemies. What made the Romans inexorable was that they had been forced to fear an enemy: when this did not happen — and it did not happen often — Rome was comparatively placable. A famous line in Virgil — *parcere subjectis et debellare superbos*, 'to spare the prostrate and break down the proud' — is a fair summary of Roman policy in war, except that the breaking down might precede the sparing. After these general reflections let us consider the foreign policy and major strategy of Rome after the Second Punic War.

What lessons did Rome learn from the Second Punic War in the field of policy and strategy? I think they learnt that it was better not to trust simply to the military strength of Rome and Italy if that could be avoided. In Spain and North Italy it was not easy to do anything else, but beyond the Adriatic Rome had found it convenient to use the Aetolians against Philip V of Macedon, and that course, economical of man power, they proposed to follow again at need. Next the Romans learnt to be uneasy about possible coalitions, such as Carthage had sought to raise up against them. They were perhaps on this account too ready to believe a little later that Macedon and Syria might make an effective combination against them. To that belief was largely due the Second Macedonian War,[10] though a contributory cause was the fear that Macedon would become a naval power (p. 36).

The opening decades of the second century brought to Rome a wide experience of diplomacy of the Hellenistic type as the Greek states strove to enlist Roman help or sympathy for their several policies and interests. When the Senate found that so much could be effected by the mere prestige of Rome or by the fact that in many matters Rome could give a disinterested judgment, it was natural that the Senate should more and more regard war as a means only to be used when less expensive means failed. The honest broker finds it easy and tempting to charge brokerage. In a world that since Alexander had more and more developed the use of arbitration, the native legalism of the Romans came to feel at home. Diplomacy was more and more a substitute for military action. On the other hand, when the Senate decided that Perseus of Macedon was a danger, their military action was preceded by careful diplomatic preparation.

Thus we find foreign policy now as a substitute for war, now as a preparation for war. We also find the use of prestige and the temptation to be overmuch governed by the claims of prestige, and by jealousy of the strength, and even of the self-respect, of other powers. This is particularly to be seen in Roman policy towards Syria. In her final dealings with Rhodes Rome's diplomacy was malevolent, and her policy was shortsighted. As was pointed out in an

earlier lecture, Rome had ceased to keep up a strong
naval power, and although the weakening of Rhodes
brought gain to Delos and so indirectly to Italian
traders at Delos,[11] Rome lost by not allowing a strong
naval power to police the waters of the Levant. The
next century was to show how unwise it was not to
keep Rhodes strong, the more as the interests of
Rhodes really ran parallel to those of Rome.

In Spain it was a defect of Roman policy that the
line of fair dealing and conciliation as practised by
the ablest Romans such as the father of the Gracchi
was not patiently followed.[12] Small as was the real
danger to Rome of the Spanish wars, they were a
drain on the man power and economic strength of
Italy, and they did much to undermine the loyalty
of the Italian allies to Rome. The destruction of
Carthage was a crime; the destruction of Corinth,
though it served its purpose of breaking the spirit
of the Greeks, must have left bitterness which came
to the surface at the time of the Mithridatic Wars;
the destruction of Numantia was effective as a
deterrent to Spanish recalcitrance and disorder, but
a wiser policy might have prevented Spain two generations later from supporting Sertorius. The siege of
Carthage and the siege of Numantia both showed
the tenacious military resourcefulness of Rome; the
campaign that ended with the fall of Corinth began
with a striking example of the use a Roman general
could make of the faulty strategy of an enemy,[13] but
it cannot be said that these events show a truly

judicious combination of foreign policy and warlike action.

Of course the responsibility for this does not lie with Rome alone. Where force and narrow self-interest rule, States may be only as wise and peaceful as other States allow them to be. The personal factors of men on the spot also play their parts. It seems to have been in the nature of Marcius to lead the Rhodians to their ruin, in the nature of Popillius Laenas to be more high-handed than was necessary in dealing with Syria. In Africa Jugurtha brought his fate upon himself by making any composition impossible, and in a way forced Rome to a policy unwelcome to the Senate and to military activity when all her forces were needed in the North. A shrewd and honest policy might indeed have kept off invading Cimbri and Teutoni, a danger to free Gaul and Spain rather than to provincial Gaul and Italy, but when that policy was not used, only a decision by arms remained, and military necessity forced on Rome military changes which were hard to adapt to the conventions of the Roman Senatorial State. The imperfections of our records for Roman history at the close of the second and beginning of the first century obscure the strategic policy of Rome, and the play of political factors and personal ambitions confused what policy there was.

The alienation of Italian allies presently brought Rome face to face with the political and military problems of the Social War. Marius, who knew that the military strength of Rome needed the conciliation rather than the destruction of the Italians, pursued a defensive that was not justly appreciated by the Senate (p. 60). The course of the war resembles in many respects that of the Samnite wars, but the danger from Mithridates and the survivals of political wisdom induced a settlement, even if partial and grudging, that placed at the disposal of Rome once more the main strength of the Italian peninsula. But even so the rift in the Roman State embodied in the clash of rival factions forced Sulla to deal with Mithridates as best he could with one eye on affairs in Italy. Also Rome had more and more to rely on the skill and prestige of generals who might provide armies and provide for them. The co-ordination of Roman strategy by the Senate becomes more and more difficult, though it did not wholly disappear. The operations of Marcus Lucullus towards the Black Sea may well have been shrewdly connected with the operations in Asia Minor of his greater brother (p. 63). The more professional, more homogeneous legions of the new model undoubtedly became more effective than Roman armies had been, and this could make up for errors in policy. Pompey was allowed to mobilize the naval strength of the Mediterranean against the pirates and to complete in his settlement of the East the effective control of the Mediterranean coasts (p. 39). Here perhaps for the last time in the history of the Roman Republic we find military and political activity working together. The failure of Pompey — his one failure — to reach a secure *modus vivendi* with Parthia left a problem which Crassus apparently sought to solve in the wrong way, so that there remained the need to re-establish Roman prestige.

The conquest of Northern Spain and the mastery of the Alps were either not envisaged or were postponed by political distractions. Whether Caesar's conquest of Gaul really added to the security and strength of Rome is debatable. But in the course of it there was trained the best army Rome ever had, in the hands of Rome's greatest master of war. The strategy of the Civil Wars is, in the main, personal, that is the forces were in the hands of eminent generals who directed the strategy as well as the tactics of their campaigns, and will be reserved for the next lecture, which will deal with generalship.

Now to sum up: I have sought to give a review of the interaction of Roman foreign policy and strategy, and it suggests to me that we should be loth, for most of Roman history, to attribute to Rome a constant, logical, foreign or strategic policy. It is true that Roman policy is on the whole pedestrian, that Rome moves more like a rook or bishop at chess, and less like the knight with its pleasing way of leaping on to the next square but one of a different colour. The outward extension of Roman power is on the whole steadily persistent, and this gives to it an air of continued purpose. But if one looks more closely, one will see that in Roman policy there is often an element of improvisation on the one hand and on the other a readiness to halt and see if problems would solve themselves. In Spain, for instance, Rome's policy was almost hand-to-mouth in the second century, and though in her Eastern policy in the same century one can detect the gradual elimination first of one power and then of another, this seems rather forced on Rome than sought by her. At times Rome seems to be philhellene, not in the sense of wishing to preserve the Greeks as they were, but of giving them credit for the greatness of an older Greece that educated Romans admired.[14] This is in part due to the influence of personalities which is not to be wholly discounted on the score that the Senate at that time effectively guided Roman policy. For among the aristocratic groups that composed the Senate, persons and families could still affect policy.

The Senate also had to act on the information it possessed, and at times it seems to have been misled by interested powers, so that on better information policy had to be reversed. Roman policy towards Macedon seems to have shifted at times for this reason. In the last century of the Republic preoccupation with domestic politics, the ambitions of generals, the intervention of the People or of the capitalists might make policy less rational or less continuous. It looks, for instance, as though the Senate misjudged the situation in Gaul as between her allies, the Aedui, the new invaders, the Helvetii, and the old invader Ariovistus; and it looks as if the

H

ambitious purpose of Caesar led to a policy of expansion which to Rome, a Mediterranean power, was not in the logic of the situation. The 'letter of Mithridates,' given in Sallust's *Histories*,[15] may very well portray Roman policy as Mithridates must have seen it at the time. It describes the Romans as remorselessly advancing from the destruction of one monarch to the destruction of the next, and yet in the event the Romans did not wholly abandon their system of client kingdons.

What I have said about foreign policy is in a measure true of strategy. It is to be remembered that Rome did not possess what modern States possess, a General Staff of highly trained soldiers to study during peace the military problems presented by any State in which or against which Rome might have to make war. It is true that in Polybius [16] Aemilius Paullus is made to say, 'the one amusement of some people, in their social gatherings, and as they strolled abroad, was how to manage the war in Macedonia, while they stayed at Rome, sometimes blaming what the generals did, and sometimes expounding their omissions.' This was more than the civilian strategy-mongering that we find so tempting nowadays, for the Roman gentry were men of some experience of war, but it falls far short of providing the means for a planned, forward-looking, strategical policy. Thus there was in general some lack of co-ordination to carry out a far-reaching strategical scheme. It is not possible to say just how serious was the danger from

Parthia three years after the defeat of Crassus at Carrhae, but the despatches of Cicero as governor of Cilicia show how little the Senate had provided for fruitful co-operation between him and his neighbour the governor of Syria.[17] Partisan or personal considerations were at times allowed to override strategic wisdom.

Furthermore, a central strategic reserve of a few legions posted in Italy always ready to be moved to any point where danger threatened would have been of great help to the Republic, but the Republic refused to solve the political and economic difficulties in the way. Even when the Empire brought a real, standing army, Augustus, in his anxiety to maintain the civilian colour of the Principate, did not post his reserve where it was most handy, that is, in North Italy, but was apt to keep it really in Spain or to move troops from one point to another.[18] This he and his immediate successors could do, because in general the initiative lay with Rome. This was not wholly true of the Republic, and the Republic can be criticized for not adapting its major strategical policy to the position created by the great expansion of Roman power in the last half century of the Republic.

There was then bound to be some lack of logical consequence in Roman foreign and military policy, and some improvisation, but, through it all, there was present a sound military instinct, a mixture of patience and boldness, an adaptation of ends to means that kept the balance of success inclining to

Rome as it never inclined for long to any other ancient State. Rome did owe a great deal, not only to her instinct for war, to her man power and its military organization, but also on occasion to the eminent skill of her generals.

The study of Roman generalship is not the study of military *expertise* in a vacuum: it is conditioned by the character of the Roman State and of the Roman soldiers. Nor is it simply the study of a few outstanding personalities, for what we need to appreciate is the whole effect of Roman generalship. But the personalities are significant, and I shall try not only to deal with the question as a whole, but to characterize the strategical skill of some of the leading figures in the military history of the Republic.

V

GENERALSHIP

IN THE previous lectures I have tried to state the problems that called for solution by the art of war as practised by the Romans of the Republic, and to set out what seem to be the character of Roman armies and fleets, the Roman attitude towards the land and the sea as the setting of warfare, and the interaction of policy and strategy, in the widest sense. All this supplies the frame within which Roman generalship is set. Yet generalship is never the whole of the picture within that frame: when we say that a general won a battle, we are using what is often a misleading simplification. History contains far more soldiers' battles than most history books would have us suppose. Also, success is not the sole and sufficient criterion of generalship. 'Mediocre generals have often beaten good generals, but that does not mean that good generals are not better than mediocre ones.'[1] Still it is possible to overrate the importance in war of generalship on a high plane. Expert students of military matters, often themselves generals and often concerned to train generals, are apt to incline this way. But Clausewitz himself has written: 'There is such a thing as military virtue. This is for the parts what the genius of the commander is for the whole.'[2] The virtue of the parts may largely compensate for lack of genius in the commander, and this is true of Rome. The military virtue of peoples may vary. Jomini [3] cites a Spanish proverb, 'He was a brave man that day,' which implies that few men are brave men every day, and adds, 'Nobody could compare the French at Rosbach with the French at Jena.' Variation is possible, but the Romans under the Republic seem to have suffered this variation less than most peoples, and their military virtue was pretty consistent. But it may be said that the constitution of the early and middle Republic provided generals who were not soldiers first and last: the Roman *imperium* confers powers and duties that do not only belong to war. This is true, but a Roman general in the field had a non-civilian plenitude of powers. No tribune could harry him, and the tremendous powers of the *imperium* backed by Roman discipline gave him a very ample sense of authority.

The dual command provided by two consuls, who are equal and may be opposite, carried with it the dangers of divided counsels in the field. This did exist, but the Romans were not unconscious of it and avoided its worst effects by rarely combining the armies of two consuls and by having, during most of the early and middle Republic, the institution of the dictatorship, which in dangerous times could give to one man an overriding authority. And when the military dictatorship was dropped the authority of the Senate in part took its place, and also the way generals now came to be appointed prevented any dual command of the same army.

It is also true that the actual command of Roman
armies in the early and middle Republic was vested
in magistrates and ex-magistrates and so was in the
main a by-product of an election which might be
concerned with matters other than purely military.
The President of the United States is Commander-
in-Chief, and he is elected for qualities other than
military skill, but then the President never expects to
take the field, even if an Abraham Lincoln can do
much to guide the fortunes of a war. A Roman
consul or proconsul, on the other hand, did become
an active general. But it is to be remembered that
the Romans were more preoccupied with war than
most modern peoples usually are: they did not leave
it to a professional hierarchy, and though they might
elect men of no military capacity, they were less
likely to do so than States in which non-military
qualities are the most appropriate means to secure
office.

But of course the proof of the pudding is in the
eating. What we have to consider is how far Roman
generals were mediocre or worse, and how far it mattered to Rome if they were. Some armies suffer less
from the mediocrity of their generals than others,
and some military systems demand less of their generals than others. If you place on one side the tend-
ency towards mediocrity of the Roman methods of
appointing commanders and on the other the high
average success which the Republic achieved in the
field, the natural conclusion is that Roman armies

and the Roman system did not require too much of their generals. Professional soldiers who have written on the art of war find it hard to dissemble their surprise at the military success which Rome achieved down to the last decades of the Republic. They are prepared to grant isolated instances of military genius or high talent among the Romans, but they attribute to the ordinary general of the Republic an amateurishness which, in their view, leaves him ill fitted to command with success.

For centuries the normal Roman commander was a magistrate or ex-magistrate in the thirties or forties, who had seen a very few years of military service perhaps in no campaign of moment, whose preoccupations had been civilian in the main, who usually had little if any knowledge of formulated military science and no more training than he could derive from generals of his own family or generals under whom he may have served. Polybius in one of his drastic moments writes thus about the generals of the Achaean League.

There are three methods followed by those who would arrive at an intelligent knowledge of generalship. The first is by the study of memoirs and the devices to be learnt from them, the second by the use of scientific treatises composed by specialists, the third by actual experience in the field. But of all three of these methods the Achaean commanders were equally ignorant. [4]

As far as the evidence allows us to judge, Roman generals had on the whole little experience of the first

two of these methods down to the first century B.C.,
and the ordinary Roman praetor or consul cannot
have had very much of the third. Towards the close
of the second century Marius mocked at the sprigs of
the nobility who were prepared to lead armies after
reading some Greek treatise on tactics, and this suggests that manuals were in vogue.[5] It is also possible
to find in the *Strategemata* of Frontinus military devices used by Roman generals in the first century
which repeat the devices of Greek commanders, but
that need not be conscious imitation. I may add by
the way that, if you analyse the military devices
given by Frontinus, the more imaginative of them are
those of non-Romans, not of Romans. During the
last century of the Republic we find a marked increase in the practice of using *legati*, that is of generals outside the normal command derived from the
tenure of a magistracy. This gave experienced soldiers
an extra chance of employment. But until the latest
decades of the Republic Rome rarely had an abundance of generals of proved high talent in the field,
based upon training and long experience.

This was not in itself altogether a disadvantage.
Generals can be too old, and the Romans usually
avoided having old men as generals. Few States have
not suffered from employing generals who in youth
had showed boldness and decision and in old age
proved hesitant and mediocre:[6] Rome seems to have
been among those few. In later military history few
generals achieved great success without a long pro-

fessional training behind them. One can think of
Cromwell, Wallenstein and Condé, but I can remember few others. There have been good generals as
young as the usual Roman commander but rarely
without being devoted to arms from their earliest
youth; Alexander the Great, Hannibal and Napoleon
had served an apprenticeship in arms before they
commanded an army.

It will be admitted that military experience alone
does not make a general. Frederick the Great observed that a mule might have made twenty campaigns under Prince Eugène and not be a better
tactician for all that. The hierarchical character of
modern armies makes long service almost a prerequi-
site for high command. Where it is realized that
generals can be too old, they are nowadays reinforced
by Chiefs of Staff who may be comparatively young,
but these are highly specialized soldiers. The Roman
general had not a Chief of Staff, and his *consilium* did
not decide for him. To entrust an army to the leading
of men of the age of the usual Roman praetor or
consul would seem to be highly hazardous. Of course
Roman generals who had shown exceptional capacity
were apt to be employed again especially at times of
crisis, but far less often than would be the case in a
modern State. On the other hand one of the capaci-
ties that experience often brings is that of steady
coolness, and where experience was lacking this quality was often supplied by the very steadiness and
firmness of the Roman character.

We must then consider what was it that a Roman general must bring to his army apart from his usually aristocratic rank, the dignity of his present or recent office and sometimes a family tradition of success, and what his army could supply to make good any deficiencies in him. Roman operations down to the last decades of the Republic were apt to be simple in tactics and strategy. To Jomini, for example, the directing principle of tactical, as of strategic, combination is to bring the main body of one's forces against one part only of the enemy and against the point which promises most results. Clausewitz declares that without a turning movement a battle could not end in complete victory. In general, Roman traditional battle tactics did not lend themselves to anything more than a parallel battle, and Roman armies rarely enjoyed the numerical superiority which is almost necessary for a turning operation. To this generalization the tactics developed by Scipio Africanus afford an exception, but his tactical ideas seem to have been almost wholly forgotten in the next century. A further exception is supplied under the late Republic, when the superior effectiveness of veteran legions was fully recognized, for the practice of concentrating veterans on one wing gave something of the effect of a flank attack.

But it remains true that for most of Roman military history battles were fought and won with simple tactics and simple strategy. To achieve results by such means a Roman army was usually well suited.

Even before the Roman army assumed a professional character the centurions could supply an experienced steady skill in the tactics of the day. In the contingents of the Italian allies the subordinate tactical command must have been efficient so as to admit of manoeuvre by the side of the legions, and when the Italian allies fought Rome in the Social War they could produce generals who made a good showing against any but the best Roman commanders. It may be assumed that the military virtues of the legions were shared by the allied contingents. At least the Roman tradition as reflected in Livy did not put upon the allies the blame for Roman reverses, as it presumably would have done were it not unreasonable to do so. Roman tactics, further, did not lend themselves to victory through that lightning perception of an opportunity which, so long as battles were on a scale that admitted of it, has been a quality of all great generals and the greatest quality of some of them. Where initiative usually was needed was in the decision when to accept battle, a choice which Roman methods sought to keep within the control of Roman generals. How important this seemed to them may be deduced from the treatment of this topic which Livy presumably took over from the earlier Roman writers whose works were before him as he wrote. In such a considered judgment shrewdness, assisted, it may be, by the advice of experienced subordinates, played a greater part than the rapid schooled decision of a great commander. In the field of strategy a general unsure of himself could usually play for time with the comfortable knowledge that a day would come, if not for him, at least for his successor. When Roman military criticism was harsh, it was harsh in judging those generals who engaged in battles beyond their skill.

The faults of Roman generals and admirals are sometimes those of inexperience, more commonly the failure to discover new tactics to meet either unfamiliar tactics or some unusual situation. The wrong deduction might be drawn from earlier battles. At the battle of the river Trebia 10,000 Romans succeeded in breaking through the Carthaginian line and escaping when the rest were destroyed. The Romans drew the deduction that Hannibal was to be defeated by massing troops for a thrust of greater weight, and this led to the defeat of Cannae because, if the advance of the Romans could be checked, the greater their numbers the less their fighting power once they were jammed together. Yet the Romans were not slow to learn from defeats, and their man power relatively to the size of each of their armies enabled them to endure this rough teaching. Failure of nerve in Roman generals seems to have been comparatively rare, but it did sometimes happen. Overconfidence combined with an imperfect intelligence service and bad scouting was a more frequent cause of defeat. Sometimes, though rarely, Roman armies were swept away in panic. A few problems, particularly that of dealing with the attack of cavalry with missiles, were not wholly solved by the Republic.

But what matters most is to consider not why the Roman generals failed when they did — a topic on which the evidence is not as abundant as we could wish — but why they succeeded so often, and I will turn to that with reference to the achievements of particular generals and try to judge them.

Rome must have had some good generals in the early period. The tradition where it can be trusted shows that some generals were successful in conditions in which other generals failed. During the Samnite Wars we can detect one great strategic stroke, the march of Fabius Rullianus through the difficult country of the Ciminian forest which brought him unexpectedly on to the flank of Rome's Etruscan enemies.[7] This may have been due to the instructions of the Senate since Fabius started from Rome, but as the same Fabius was one of the two generals who led the Roman armies to a decisive strategic point before the battle of Sentinum he may well have been the author of both movements and, if so, a man of strategic vision.[8] In the war with Pyrrhus it looks as if the Roman generals were quick to learn how to counter the tactical skill of their opponent.

But on the whole we cannot discover accurately wherein the merit of Roman generals lay until we reach the Second Punic War. The first Roman commander, in fact, of whom it can be said with certainty

that he added something to the art of war was Scipio
Africanus. He has been declared 'a greater than
Napoleon,'[9] but that is an exaggeration. As a
strategist he was far more daring than any other
Roman general of the middle Republic, and his daring was rewarded with success. But I am inclined to
think that he owed more to the incompetence of the
enemy or the battle qualities of his troops than to
his own strategic judgment. He failed to pin down
Hannibal's brother to Spain, which was one task
that it was his prime duty to carry out. In Africa
his bold march inland before the decisive battle
with Hannibal has been both praised and blamed by
military critics:[10] myself, I am inclined to think that
the blame is juster than the praise. But in tactics
he was an innovator of great merit, even if his tactics
were the application to Roman technique of ideas
learnt from Hannibal's early victories. It is indeed
fascinating to observe how he added to the holding
attack along the line the flank movement which Hannibal had so brilliantly exploited.[11] I believe that in
the final battle at Zama Hannibal saw through his
tactics and found the right counter, and the Roman
victory was due rather to the fighting qualities of the
Roman troops than to Scipio's skill. Except for one
thing. What made the victory certain was the control Scipio had of his men, and for this control, which
went beyond that of the normal Roman general,
Scipio must have the credit. He had, it is true, advantages that no other Roman general had hitherto

I

enjoyed, in a long command of the same army during which he could train it and train himself in warfare against good—but not very good—generals. It is right to remember that at Zama he had had a longer experience of handling troops than Hannibal possessed when he fought the Trebia, Trasimene and Cannae. But when all allowances are made, Scipio was a great general, and when he died he left behind him no one who could do what he had done.

Indeed, so far as we can tell, Rome produced few really good generals in the second century. It is true that during the first half of the century the Romans won three great battles, Cynoscephalae, Magnesia and Pydna. In the first of these, however, the Aetolians claimed to have played the decisive part and may have done so; the second victory was due to the initiative of Eumenes, King of Pergamum, who was fighting with the Romans. About Pydna we know hardly anything. It may be that the battle was lost by the Macedonian King rather than won by the Roman general, but the smallness of the Roman losses, if the tradition may be trusted, suggests competent handling of the Roman army.[12] In the second half of the second century Rome produced an exceptional crop of bad generals and very few good ones. The younger Scipio, the conqueror of Carthage and Numantia, was at least a good organizer. Metellus in the war with Jugurtha may have really solved the problem of that war before the command was transferred to Marius.[13] Marius not only was a great military reformer but must have been a good tactician, and, to judge from the campaign against the Cimbri and Teutoni, a sound strategist. The ancient evidence is incomplete, but it suffices to show that he was a master in defensive tactics when they were needed. When in the Social War an Italian commander said, 'If you are a great general, come down and fight me,' Marius anticipated Turenne by saying, 'If you are a great general, come and make me fight you.' [14]

But to pass to the first century, I am inclined to think that the greatest general Rome produced after Scipio Africanus was Sulla, the first great master of the new school of Roman tacticians. In the Social War he won victories where other experienced generals failed; at Chaeronea in Greece, he seems to have shown the resource and quickness of eye which mark out the great commander in the field. How far he is responsible for the greater flexibility and thrust that enters into Roman tactics it is hard to say, but it seems to have happened during his career and he may well be its true begetter. He appears, indeed, to have made war with the cold and formidable resolution that marked his political career. Sertorius, who upheld against odds a failing cause in Spain, was a pupil of Marius. He combined skill in the normal tactics of a Roman army with a keen appreciation of the advantages which Spain offers to a nimble army which can make the country and its inhabitants its allies.[15] If I am right in thinking he was a soldier of the older school, he supplied some undesired education to an able young general in Pompey and to an able older general in Metellus. But before Sulla had died Roman armies had become something they had not been before, and the character of the armies had a real effect on Roman generalship. Not only the new military quality of the army but its relation to its generals was destined to affect Roman generalship, and to that topic I must now turn.

Various causes combined to bring about this new relationship of the armies to their chiefs. The legionaries, who made arms their trade, looked to their generals rather than to the State to provide them first with employment and then with the bounties and plots of land which formed their consolidated pensions when they left the eagles. The military emergencies that filled the forty years that followed the Social War were largely met by the employment of commanders of repute who attracted soldiers to serve under them. Marius by his series of consulships, which were really generalships, and by his military reforms had pointed the way which others were to take. The army which Sulla took across the Adriatic to fight Mithridates with or without the recognition of the government at home became the instrument of his purposes. It was his army, ready to be led against those who controlled Rome; it fought for its general against whatever enemy he pointed to, and it received its reward in booty, bounties and settlements of land. Whatever Sulla might have done to secure power for the kind of Senate he thought Rome needed, the example of his career made a dangerous precedent. A world of ambitious men could not forget him — *Sulla potuit: ego non potero?* [16] But we are not concerned here with the effect of this on the State or on the legionaries so much as on the general. The new kind of general was sparing of the lives of his troops, careful of their comfort, and faced with the problem set by the need of keeping their devotion while not losing control of them. An interesting inscription of the Social War shows Pompeius Strabo rewarding Spanish cavalry that served with him. [17] Caesar's care for the political interests of Cisalpine Gaul was partly due to the fact that it was his chief recruiting ground. A judicious use of promotions and decorations could also attach the troops to their generals. A general held his command not for single campaigns but for wars covering several years in the same region. He thus became more professional, more at home with his troops, and as his military reputation became more needed for his political position, he gave attention to it. The Republic in fact was developing a breed of generals who could more and more leave their civil careers to be advanced by their agents, especially tribunes, while they devoted themselves to their armies. They needed to be successful soldiers; they also needed to be able to offer military employment to apprentices in the same trade.

They sought military employment because so they could hold their armies together. Each of the greater commanders gathered round him military aspirants who provided excellent subordinates. Lucullus had been the lieutenant of Sulla and inherited the task of dealing with Mithridates. Between the death of Sulla and the Civil War the greatest military reputation was that of Pompey, who came to have military patronage to bestow. A man like Afranius for example, who had apparently no gift for politics, looked to military employment as *legatus* of Pompey, so too did Petreius. It has recently been suggested that Labienus was lent by Pompey to Caesar.[18] The younger Crassus served under Caesar in Gaul until in a luckless hour he rejoined his father for his ill-fated Syrian expedition. Besides these there arose a group of soldiers whose careers were to be made by Caesar's own career as a general. The ramifications of Roman social influence took among other forms the form of commending men for military employment. Q. Cicero, the orator's brother, became a kind of general *malgré lui* with Caesar, because Caesar did not undervalue the political influence of the orator's golden tongue. The one eminent general of the post-Sullan period who did not pursue this policy was Lucullus. Brilliant soldier as he was, eminent alike in the new tactics and in the organization of supply, he neither trained an army to be devoted to him nor a group of officers either dependent on himself or animated by his old-fashioned loyalty to the Senate.

That his failure to keep a hold on his troops was not due wholly to their desire to return to peaceful life is shown by the fact that many of them on discharge at once re-enlisted under Pompey.[19]

The military talent of the late Republic came to be divided between the lieutenants of Pompey and the lieutenants of Caesar, between two hierarchies, though when Caesar and Pompey worked together there was, as we have seen, some cross-fertilization as it were. The same came to be true of the veteran soldiers and above all of the centurions who counted for so much for the efficiency of a Roman army.

When the Civil War broke out, the talent on the side of Pompey was on the whole greater than that on the side of Caesar, but after Caesar's lightning invasion of Italy the majority of veterans and centurions were at his disposal.[20] Caesar's genius could compensate for the slight inferiority of his detached commanders, the skill of Pompey and his lieutenants was hampered by the slight inferiority of their troops. And Pompey suffered from the fact that fighting on the side of the Senate he had to endure the weaknesses of some Senatorial officers who did not belong to the Pompeian school. The most fatal case of this was the pigheaded folly of Domitius Ahenobarbus, to which I shall refer later. On the other hand Caesar was not, I think, anything like as good a judge of soldiers as he was a soldier, and he failed to keep the loyalty of his best officers such as Trebonius and Decimus Brutus. But by then he had won his victory. More dangerous was his failure to retain Labienus, his ablest lieutenant, who deserted him at the very outbreak of the Civil War.

There is no need to admire the character of Labienus, who certainly was not a nice man for a small tea-party. But he was not only a determined and able tactician, he was in a way a general of the future. More than any other soldier of the day he appreciated the possibilities of combined cavalry and light armed troops,[21] and he was the distant forerunner of the great Roman generals of the later Empire. His idea of winning Pharsalus with cavalry was tactically sound, and would, I believe, have succeeded except against the rare combination of a general of genius and troops of the very highest skill and aggressiveness. Labienus may have left Caesar because of Caesar's advancement of Antony. Antony's one great victory, that of Philippi, is not recorded with sufficient detail to enable us to judge him as a tactician. He was bold in advance, undaunted and resourceful in retreat, a soldiers' general: but when you have said that you have said all, or at least all that can now be said.

The merits of Pompey as a general in his youth and middle age were those of speed. That this is praised by Cicero is perhaps not so significant, for to Cicero what was not a topic for invective was a topic for panegyric. But even after Pompey's death Cato is made to praise it by one of Caesar's officers in his account of the War in Africa.[22] In the engagement in which Pompey worsted Caesar at Dyrrhachium he showed great skill even if he failed to press his advantage right home. He was a good organizer and a man who could both train troops and win their affection. In politics he was cold, mean-spirited, tortuous, incapable of inspiring affection. As Cicero bitterly said of him, he was *'se ipse amans sine rivali'*; in the field he was a different man. But what marks him out most is his appreciation of amphibious warfare, of the use both of sea and land so far as ancient conditions admitted of it. In this his one rival in Roman history is Agrippa, who was both an admiral and a general, the man whose genius gave to Octavian the military success that made the Empire possible in the form it took. Agrippa is the last great Roman soldier of the Republic, and not the least.

To return to our main theme, it must be granted that professional generalship was more common and had more scope in the closing decades of the Republic than at any other time in Roman history. The Roman legionaries had always been good at field fortifications: now they were extremely skilful at all kinds of field works. This skill was used against non-Romans, as by Caesar in Gaul, and still more when the Civil Wars brought legions to meet legions. The art of avoiding battle was beginning to develop to a great height, and this largely due to a shrewd use of the terrain and of fortifications. Warfare became something more than two armies marching to meet each other, deploying for battle and fighting it out.

Campaigns were not walking tours ending in a battle. They are a continuous exposition of the art of war known at the time and combine strategical and tactical preparation of a high degree of subtlety. The fact that armies moved as it were cleared for action if not wholly without baggage gave importance to supply and set the problem of securing this without being condemned to immobility. Fortified towns were skilfully used as *points d'appui*, but Roman Republican warfare at its zenith is not a war of sieges. Apart from Rome itself — and Rome was rather the prize than the means of victory — there was hardly a city whose possession was of prime importance. Warfare of this character was a constant intellectual problem for generals and also for soldiers.

Between Roman generals and their troops there was a close contact despite, or perhaps even because of, the firmness of Roman discipline. The pages of the first decade of Livy are full of armies reproaching generals and of generals rebuking armies. This may be in the main a literary device to bring in speeches to adorn the narrative. But the contacts of generals and soldiers are too well attested later for this picture to be wholly false. A major question of judgment, as has been said, is when to accept or offer battle, and on that the generals feel that they must carry their troops' judgment with them. I do not suggest that the Livian battles of the early Republic are historical in detail — the tradition did not allow of that — but Livy's ideas about soldiers and

generals presumably reflect neither his own unaided
opinion nor even only that of the Augustan age in
which he wrote but, in great measure, the tradition
of the chain of writers going back to the middle Republic which made up the raw material of his early
Roman history.

Between the more professional troops of the late
Republic and their generals there was a kind of coincidence of expertness. In the campaign of Ilerda
Caesar's veterans were as well aware as their general of the importance of overtaking the retreating
Pompeians.[23] At Pharsalus the same veterans in-
·stinctively checked their advance when Pompey
tried to gain an advantage by leaving the Caesarians
to do all the charging.[24] At Thapsus, indeed, Caesar's
legions forced his hand by attacking when they saw
victory possible without waiting for the full deployment which their general desired.[25] The loyalty of
Roman soldiers to their generals was, in the main,
based on a shrewd appreciation of their qualities in
the field. This does not mean that Roman generals
allowed their soldiers to make decisions for them,
still less to have a dangerous knowledge of their
purposes. Caesar, for instance, would have endorsed
the dictum of Frederick, that if his night-cap knew
his plans he would throw it into the fire. But, especially in the closing decades of the Republic, generals had to earn the trust which then they used.
An excellent idea of how Roman soldiers at that time
regarded their generals may be gained from the *Bel-*

lum Africum, which is found among the works of the Caesarian corpus. Granted that Caesar was an exceptional general and his veterans exceptional troops, one can still see how a soldier of ordinary capacity, such as the writer of the *Bellum Africum*, must have regarded his general and what his general had to do to retain his strong grasp on his men. There is a certain objective professional judgment mingled with a personal admiration for Caesar. Where the troops could not know Caesar's purposes and were apparently in a situation that was anxious and dangerous they took courage when they saw Caesar's vigorous and cheerful countenance and believed that his technical skill and planning would make all things easy for them.[26] So in the Peninsular War it was said of Wellington that the sight of his long nose filled his troops with a confidence 'worth 10,000 men any day of the week.' [27] But the *Bellum Africum*, which is appreciative of the merits also of the enemy commanders, and other ancient texts show that Roman soldiers were not led by the glamour of personality but by a shrewd appreciation of military skill. The new generals of the late Republic then had to win and keep the professional respect of the new soldiers of that epoch.

It may be argued that preoccupation with the strategical and tactical preparation for battle caused a defect in appreciating the broader issues of strategy. Highly skilled professional soldiers have sometimes not seen beyond their noses, even if these are as long

as Wellington's. I am inclined to think that even
Caesar towards the end of his career came to suffer
somewhat from the limiting effect of virtuosity. It
has well been pointed out how shrewd was his broad
strategy in Gaul, his first great military experience,
how he resisted the temptation to try to be strong
everywhere and of seeking to hold Gaul by scattered
detachments.[28] Once only he spread out his legions,
and that, if we may trust him, partly because he was
forced by difficulties of supply. The result was a
disaster, though limited and quickly repaired. He
learnt from this, and in the dangerous hour of the
rising of Vercingetorix he contrived to reunite his
forces which had been divided into two. The dis-
position of his troops at the outbreak of the Civil
War with his main force still in Gaul was justified
by his brilliant conception of a surprise invasion of
Italy to be followed by an invasion of Spain where
was the one considerable army in being at the disposal of his great adversary Pompey. Pompey's dispositions, granted that Caesar's stroke prevented
him from bringing his Spanish army to Italy, were
strategically sound, and might even have been an
effective counter if Domitius Ahenobarbus had con-
formed to his first strategic plan to build up an army
in South Italy. Pompey's decision, when that failed,
to leave Italy was sound, and not less sound because
it did not commend itself to Cicero.[29] Caesar after
eliminating the Pompeian army in Spain crossed to
the Balkans to face Pompey. When Pompey had

won a victory at Dyrrhachium, his decision to follow
Caesar to Greece rather than to go to Italy was I
think justified, and I am not among those who think
that his decision to join battle at Pharsalus was a
military blunder forced on him by the aristocrats in
his camp.[30] On the whole Pompey proved himself
an excellent strategist on broad lines worthy of the
Pompey who had so swiftly and surely dealt with
the pirates. But he was the first man in his army to
be defeated at Pharsalus, and that blow may have
subjected him to the intellectual weakening that so
often befalls a man who regards himself as a pathetic
figure. I cannot believe that the Ptolemaic Kingdom
to which he fled could offer him anything but a grave.

But to return to Caesar. Up to Pharsalus he
showed great force in seizing and keeping the initiative, and judgment in not forgetting the need to
secure the food supply of Rome. The sending of a
force to Africa can be justified: what cannot be justified was the sending of Curio to command it, and
Caesar was punished for a weakness he sometimes
showed, a defective judgment of his own officers. At
Dyrrhachium he took overgreat risks, but they were
largely forced upon him. After Pharsalus, which he
won by finding a drastic answer to what was in itself
a promising tactical scheme, he rightly pursued Pompey to Alexandria. For Pompey's name was still
potent, and his death was a necessity for Caesar's
victory. But if Caesar went to Alexandria in pursuit
of Pompey, he remained in pursuit of Cleopatra, and

it is hard to believe that he could not have disengaged his army earlier than he did, whatever the length of his sojourn may have been.[31] His campaign in Asia Minor, swift though it was, meant a somewhat hazardous delay in returning to Rome. He left Africa too long to itself, and in his campaign there, after he had overcome the first difficulties, he seems to have been too interested in virtuosity, rather than in finishing off the campaign,[32] even if the march to Thapsus which tempted his enemies to battle was one of his greatest strokes. He appears to have misjudged the later situation in Spain until he went there himself to fight his last battle, and it almost seems as if he let himself become necessary, as though he allowed the disease to grow from sheer desire to apply the cure.

If Caesar is to be judged by the highest standards of statesmanship, it may have to be said that his decision to march against Parthia at the last was a triumph of the soldier in him over the statesman. But if the soldier in Caesar triumphed, it was a great soldier, worthy to stand with Alexander, Hannibal and Napoleon. His achievements were limited by his needs. He had not to conquer space like Alexander, he had not to keep the devotion of an army in a long struggle against odds like Hannibal, he had not to make far-reaching strategical combinations like Napoleon. He had not to make innovations in the art of war. In this he does not match Epaminondas, or Frederick the Great. It is even possible that Labienus had a deeper insight into the limitations of legions and the methods of handling cavalry. But if he did not make great innovations it was because he did not need to. He could play the tunes of his time on an unrivalled instrument which others had made but which he perfected. Within the range of his needs he was versatility itself, and he was incalculable. Even Napoleon ceased to be that, and the generals of the Holy Alliance learnt often to foresee and sometimes to counter his moves. But in war, as in politics, Caesar remained a riddle to his opponents.[33] It has been said of Napoleon that he thought what every grenadier in his army thought, but thought it with unexampled violence. Caesar was a soldiers' general, but he thought beyond his soldiers.

Here the matter may be left. The art of war under the Roman Republic was something that belonged to Rome, a plant that grew in Roman soil, something which needed for its application talent not genius, but in its culmination it did produce a soldier greater than itself, a soldier in whom there was that fusing together of intellect and will that marks off genius from talent.

NOTES

K

NOTES TO CHAPTER I

1. Kromayer-Veith, *Heerwesen und Kriegführung der Griechen und Römer*, pp. 1 ff.

2. E. Meyer, *Kleine Schriften* II, p. 231 f.; E. S. McCartney, *Mem. of the Amer. Acad. in Rome* I, 1917, pp. 121 ff., esp. p. 156 f.

3. For discussions of this vexed question see *e.g.* J. Kromayer, *Hermes* XXXV, 1900, pp. 200 ff.; Th. Steinwender, *Die römische Taktik zur Zeit der Manipularstellung*; H. Delbrück, *Geschichte der Kriegskunst* I³, pp. 349, 443, 436, 457; Meyer, *op. cit.*, pp. 198 ff.; Kromayer-Veith, *op. cit.*, pp. 356 ff.

4. Livy VIII, 8.

5. A. Schulten in *C. A. H.* VIII, p. 318.

6. E. Altham, *The Principles of War*, p. 410 f.

7. Polybius VI, 31, 14.

8. W. Fischer, *Das römische Lager*, pp. 134 ff.

9. Aeschylus, *Agam.* 1236.

10. An extreme example is the insistence of the veteran legio Martia at the battle of Forum Gallorum that recruit formations should not fight with them ὡς μὴ συνταράξειαν αὐτοὺς ὑπὸ ἀπειρίας. Appian, *Bell. Civ.* III, 67, 275.

11. For some exceptions see Th. Steinwender, *Philol.* XXXIX, 1880, pp. 527 ff.

12. Polybius VI, 21, 4-5.

13. This seems also to follow from the use of Italians in maniples by Pyrrhus (Polybius XVIII, 28, 10); cf. Meyer, *op. cit.*, p. 233.

14. See the speech of Sp. Ligustinus in Livy XLII, 34; cf. G. H. Stevenson in *C. A. H.* IX, p. 444 f.

15. Delbrück, *op. cit.* I³, p. 464.

16. Tacitus, *Ann.* I, 23, 4.

17. Polybius VI, 24, 9.

18. Caesar, *Bell. Civ.* III, 28, 4.

19. Kromayer-Veith, *op. cit.*, p. 377.

20. H. Last in *C. A. H.* IX, p. 136; H. M. D. Parker, *The Roman Legions*, p. 26.

21. Last, *ibid.*, IX, p. 146 f.

22. Last, *ibid.*, VII, p. 342.

23. *C. A. H.* VII, p. 589.

NOTES TO CHAPTER II

1. *History of Rome*, Eng. Trans. II, pp. 40–46; IV, p. 169.
2. Thucydides, IV, 11, 4.
3. Plutarch, *Ant.* 64, 3.
4. Tacitus, *Hist.* I, 31; cf. also *Bell. Afric.* 34, 6.
5. Cassius Dio XI, frag. 43, 9 (Boissevain); cf. Diodorus XXIII, 2.
6. πλεῖν ἀνάγκη, ζῆν οὐκ ἀνάγκη. Plutarch, *Pomp.* 50; *Apophth. Pomp.* 12; cf. E. Meyer, *Caesars monarchie²*, p. 118, n. 2. Cicero (*ad Att.* X, 8, 4) says of Pompey *cuius omne consilium Themistocleum, existimat enim qui mare teneat, eum necesse ⟨esse⟩ rerum potiri.*
7. *Bell. Alex.* 44–47; reading at 46 ... *parem esse [fortuitae] dimicationi, fortunae rem committere maluit.*
8. E. T. Salmon, *J. R. S.* XXVI, 1936, pp. 52 ff.
9. Livy VIII, 14, 12.
10. *Ibid.* VIII, 14, 8, *interdictum mari Antiati populo est.*
11. Mommsen, *Staatsrecht* II³, p. 580.
12. Polybius I, 20.
13. W. W. Tarn, *J. H. S.* XXVII, 1907, pp. 48 ff.
14. W. L. Rodgers, *Greek and Roman Naval Warfare*, pp. 319 ff.
15. G. T. Griffith, *Cambridge Hist. Journ.* V, 1, 1935, pp. 8 ff.
16. P. V. M. Benecke in *C. A. H.* VIII, p. 263.
17. Livy XL, 18, 7. 26, 8. 28, 7, 42, 8. XLI, 1, 2 ff.
18. H. A. Ormerod, *Piracy in the Ancient World*, p. 187.
19. *Supp. Epig. Graec.* III, 378.
20. Bloch-Carcopino, *Hist. Rom.* II, pp. 341 ff.
21. Salmon, *loc. cit.*
22. Livy XL, 28, 7.
23. *Ibid.* XLV, 43, 10.
24. J. Kromayer, *Philol.* LVI, 1897, pp. 470 ff.
25. *Ibid.*, p. 475 f.
26. Ormerod, *J. R. S.* XII, 1922, pp. 35 ff.
27. J. Dobiáš, *Archiv Orientalni* III, 2, 1931, pp. 244 ff.
28. Kromayer, *op. cit.*, pp. 429 ff.
29. W. W. Tarn in *C. A. H.* X, p. 100; *J. R. S.* XXI, 1931, pp. 173 ff.
30. *C. A. H.* V, p. 195; A. W. Gomme, *Essays in Greek History and Literature*, pp. 192 ff. Tarn, *Hellenistic Naval and Military Developments*, pp. 124, 142.

31. Rodgers, *op. cit.*, p. 348; cf. the operations of Antony which defeated the blockade of Brundisium by Libo, Caesar, *Bell. Civ.* III, 24.

32. Diodorus XX, 112.

33. W. D. Bird, *The Direction of War*, p. 67.

34. Mahan, *op. cit.*, p. 22.

35. Tarn, *op. cit.*, p. 131.

36. Tarn, *J. H. S.* XXVII, 1907, p. 51, n. 19.

NOTES TO CHAPTER III

1. *C. A. H.* VII, p. 595 f.

2. *Ibid.*, pp. 611 ff.

3. T. Frank in *C. A. H.* VII, p. 688; for Dionysius cf. Diodorus XIV, 55, 5.

4. Republican history affords little evidence of epidemics in Roman armies, and this points to good sanitary discipline. On the other hand, the Republic does not seem to have possessed any army medical service, even if some high officers were accompanied by their own personal physicians (Suetonius, *Div. Aug.* 11).

5. A. Schulten in *C. A. H.* VIII, pp. 313, 317.

6. Schulten, *Sertorius*, pp. 107, 118 ff.

7. R. Syme in *C. A. H.* X, p. 355.

8. H. Last, *ibid.*, IX, pp. 148 ff.

9. E. Sadée, *Rhein. Mus.* LXXXVIII, 1939, p. 43.

10. R. Gardner in *C. A. H.* IX, p. 197.

11. Last, *ibid.*, IX, pp. 272 ff.

12. G. Veith, *Geschichte der Feldzüge C. Julius Caesars*, pp. 231 ff.

13. H. A. Ormerod in *Piracy in the Ancient World*, p. 177.

14. G. H. Stevenson, *Roman Provincial Administration*, p. 78 f.

15. Cicero, *in Pison.* 16, 38.

16. Horace, *Ep.* II, 2, 26 ff. (I was reminded of this passage by Prof. A. D. Nock).

17. T. Rice Holmes, *Caesar's Conquest of Gaul²*, pp. 11, 16 ff.

18. H. Delbrück, *Geschichte der Kriegskunst* I³, pp. 548 ff.

19. Caesar, *Bell. Gall.* I, 2; Syme in *C.A.H.* X, p. 348.

20. W. W. Tarn, *ibid.*, IX, pp. 607 ff.; F. Lammert, *Philol. Suppl.* XXIII, 2, 1931.

21. Syme, *ibid.*, X, p. 352.

22. M. P. Charlesworth, *ibid.*, X, pp. 84 ff.; Syme, *ibid.*, X, p. 355 f.; E. Swoboda, *Octavian und Illyricum*.

23. G. Säflund, *Le mura di Roma reppublica*, p. 173 f.; cf. I. A. Richmond in *J. R. S.* XXII, 1932, p. 235 f.

24. Lehmann-Hartleben in P. W. *s.v.* Städtebau, col. 2052 and Säflund, *op. cit.*, pp. 187 ff.; cf. Appian. *Bell. Civ.* I, 66, 303.

25. Caesar, *Bell. Civ.* III, 58, 1.

26. Auct. anon. 'Caesar's Art of War and of Writing' in *The Atlantic Monthly*, XLIV, 1879, p. 282.

NOTES TO CHAPTER IV

1. *C.A.H.* VII, p. 585 f.

2. See particularly H. Delbrück, *Geschichte der Kriegskunst* I³ *passim*, with the criticisms of J. Kromayer, *Hist. Zeit.* CXXXI, 1925, pp. 393 ff.

3. T. Frank in *C. A. H.* VII, p. 683.

4. B. L. Hallward in *C. A. H.* VIII, p. 31.

5. *Ibid.*, p. 33.

6. *Ibid.*, pp. 60 ff.

7. *Ibid.*, p. 96.

8. Polybius, XXXVIII, 22; 2.

9. Jomini, *Précis de l'art de la guerre*, p. 144.

10. M. Holleaux in *C. A. H.* VIII, p. 158; see also (for the view that the agreement between Philip and Antiochus was a Rhodian fabrication) D. Magie in *J. R. S.* XXIX, 1939, pp. 32 ff., and the literature cited *ibid.*, p. 34, n. 10.

11. M. Rostovtzeff in *C. A. H.* VIII, p. 644.

12. A. Schulten, *ibid.*, VIII, p. 314.

13. P. V. M. Benecke, *ibid.*, VIII, p. 303.

14. Holleaux, *ibid.*, VIII, p. 159.

15. Sallust, *Hist.* IV, 69 ed. Maurenbrecher.

16. Polybius, XXIX, 1, 1; cf. Livy, XLIV, 22, 8; Plutarch, *Aemilius*, 11.

17. Cicero, *ad Fam.* XV, 1 and 2.

18. *C. A. H.* X, p. 598 f.

NOTES TO CHAPTER V

1. Jomini, *Précis de l'art de la guerre*, p. 90.

2. Clausewitz, *On war*, trans. Graham, ed. Maude, I, p. 152.

3. *Op. cit.*, p. 617; cf. Wellington's judgment of his army after Talavera, 'with an army which a fortnight ago beat double their numbers I should now hesitate to meet a French corps of half their strength.'

4. Polybius XI, 8, 1–3.

5. Sallust, *Jugurtha*, 85, 12; cf. Cicero, *ad Fam.* IX, 25, 1.

6. E.g. Beaulieu, Benedek, Bazaine, Buller, Melas, Mack (cited by Col. Maude in Clausewitz, *op. cit.*, I, p. 188).

7. *C. A. H.* VII, p. 605.

8. *Ibid.*, p. 611 f.

9. B. H. Liddell Hart, *A Greater than Napoleon; Scipio Africanus.*

10. E.g. K. Lehmann, *Jahr. Phil. Suppl.* XXI, 1894; H. Delbrück, *Geschichte der Kriegskunst* I³, p. 406; G. Veith, *Antike Schlachtfelder*, III, 2, pp. 638 ff.; *ibid.*, IV, pp. 626 ff.

11. H. H. Scullard, *Scipio Africanus in the Second Punic War*, p. 138.

12. P. V. M. Benecke in *C. A. H.* VIII, p. 270.

13. M. Holroyd, *J. R. S.* XVIII, 1928, pp. 1 ff.

14. Plutarch, *Marius*, 33, 4.

15. See A. Schulten, *Sertorius.*

16. Cicero, *ad Att.* IX, 10, 2.

17. Dessau *I. L. S.* 8888; G. H. Stevenson, *J. R. S.* IX, 1919, pp. 95 ff.; C. Cichorius, *Römische Studien*, pp. 130 ff.

18. R. Syme, *J. R. S.* XXVIII, 1938, pp. 113 ff.

19. Cassius Dio XXXVI, 16, 3; cf. H. Last in *C. A. H.* IX, p. 136.

20. *C. A. H.* IX, pp. 647, 899.

21. F. Lammert, *Philol. Suppl.* XXIII, 2, 1931.

22. *Bell. Afric.* 22, 2.

23. Caesar, *Bell. Civ.* I, 64, 3.

24. *Ibid.*, III, 93, 1.

25. *Bell. Afric.* 82, 2–4.

26. *Ibid.*, 10, 2–4.

27. W. D. Bird, *The Direction of War*, p. 298.

28. Delbrück, *op. cit.*, pp. 548 ff.

29. *C. A. H.* IX, pp. 644 ff.

30. *Ibid.*, IX, p. 664 f.

31. L. E. Lord, *J. R. S.* XXVIII, 1938, pp. 13 ff.

32. *Bell. Afric.* 73.

33. *The Atlantic Monthly*, XLIV, 1879, p. 278.

INDEX

INDEX

Actium, battle of, 4, 30f., 41f., 43

Adriatic, 47; in Civil War, 40; piracy in, 37, 63

Aedui, relations with Rome, 59, 63

Aemilius, L. Paullus (*cos.* 182, 168 B.C.), 94

Aequi, wars with Rome, 51f.

Aetolians, allies of Rome, 87; at Cynoscephalae, 110

Afranius, L. (*cos.* 60 B.C.), 114

Africa, in Roman wars, 47, 55, 66, 81; Roman annexations in, 62

Agrigentum, in First Punic War, 55

Agrippa, M. Vipsanius, 39, 41f.; and sea power, 117

Alexander the Great, 12, 40, 64, 71, 104, 123

Allia, battle of, 7

Allies, *see under* Italy

Alps, 66; Dinaric, 59; Maritime, 58f.; passes, 65f.

Antiochus the Great, 36f.

Antium, fleet of, 32

Antony, 30; generalship of, 116; in Civil War, 40ff.; in Parthia, 66, 71

Aquileia, 59f.

Archers, 25f.

Ariminum, 62

Ariovistus, Senate and, 93

Asculum, siege and battle of, 61

Asia, Roman province, 64

—— Minor, 47; Roman policy towards, 64f.

Augustus and Roman army, 4f., 22; in Alps, 66; in Balkans, 67; in Spain, 58; military policy of, 95

Austerlitz, battle of, 78

Balkan peninsula, Augustus' policy in, 67; Republican policy in, 63, 80f.

Bellum Africum, 116, 119f.

Bibulus, M. Calpurnius (*cos.* 59 B.C.), admiral of Pompey, 40

Black Sea, piracy in, 42

Blockade, ancient, limitations of, 43f.

Brasidas, 29

Bremen, Haus Seefahrt, 31

Brundisium, 61, 63

Brutus, Decimus Junius, and Caesar, 115

Brutus, M. Junius, 41

Byzantium, 67

Caesar, C. Julius, 19, 26, 61, 70f.; generalship of, 121ff.; in Civil War, 62, 77, 115f., 117, 119, 121ff.; in Gallic War, 94, 117, 121; soldiers' general, 120, 124

Camps, Roman, 13ff., 69, 84; moral effect of, 14

Campania, Campanians, and Rome, 23, 33, 52f., 54, 61